Tavern Treasures

A BOOK OF PUB COLLECTABLES

Charles E Tresise

Tavern Treasures

A BOOK OF PUB COLLECTABLES

Charles E Tresise

TX
912
T73
1983

First published in the U.K. 1983 by
Blandford Press, Link House, West Street,
Poole, Dorset, BH15 1LL

Distributed in the United States by
Sterling Publishing Co., Inc., 2 Park Avenue,
New York, N.Y. 10016

British Library Cataloguing in Publication Data

Tresise, Charles E.
  Tavern treasures.
  1. Hotels, taverns, etc.—Furnishing,
  equipment, etc.—Collectors and collecting
  I. Title
  647'.95   TX912

ISBN 0 7137 1192 2

Typeset by August Filmsetting, Warrington,
Cheshire
Printed by Butler & Tanner, Frome, Somerset

Contents

I am indebted to so large a number of friends and business associates for invaluable help in compiling this book that to acknowledge each one by name would read like the Debrett of the Brewing World!

Wherever possible I have mentioned the source of photographs and prints, and of extracts from books and articles, so may I please be forgiven for any omissions? The bibliography has been arranged under chapter headings to provide an easy reference for those wishing to pursue further research.

Acknowledgements

Many of the photographs in this book were provided by the author, Charles E. Tresise. Other sources, not credited in the text, which the author and publisher gratefully acknowledge, are listed below.

Photographs

Mrs Ivy Grant: p.22; Terry Keegan/The Country Centre, Clows Top: p.115 (*bis*); *Lancashire Evening Post*: p.16; Paul Ley: p.31; Lincolnshire Museums: p.117; Penelope Mansell-Jones/Christie's: pp.68–69, 74; National Horse Brass Society: p.92; Gordon Pollock Collection: p.103; Poole Museums Service: p.130; Royal Doulton Collectors' Club: p.33; Royal Doulton Potteries: p.111; Mr & Mrs Scriven/The Three Horseshoes: p.90; Showerings, Shepton Mallett: pp.86–87; Sotheby's: p.28.

Line Illustrations

Acton Scott Working Museum: pp.113, 120; Bass Museum (from Bass & Co. Ltd as described in *Noted Breweries of Great Britain and Ireland* by Alfred Barnard republished 1977): p.47; Bickerdyke, J. (1899) *The Curiosities of Ale & Beer*: pp.23, 25; David Dowland: pp.99, 119; Fletcher, E. (1979) *Bottle Collecting* Blandford Press: pp.19, 20 (*bis*); Museum of Brewing: p.37.

Foreword

Zeppelin FH3 droned smoothly above Burton upon Trent at 5000 ft and 30 knots, on a night in 1916. The Captain had tried to reach Liverpool, but navigational errors brought him back over Burton, with its dozens of breweries and 56 miles of railway sidings. A brilliant overhead gas-light at the town-centre crossroads could not be extinguished because the man who held the key was missing. People desperately threw bricks at it until the Chairman of the Gas Company was discovered, with the lamp key, in the nearby Liberal Club. But too late! The bomb-aimer had fixed his sights and down whistled a stick of 100-kilogram bombs, hitting the Christ Church Mission Hall on the corner and killing fifteen people. Shortly afterwards I was born at our home not far away; later there was another Zeppelin alert. We were whisked away to nearby Tutbury Castle, where I spent the first few days of my life in the dungeons beneath, where Mary Queen of Scots had been imprisoned. She had had regular supplies of beer supplied from Burton Abbey of which it was said:

'The Abbott of Burton brewed good ale
On Fridays when they fasted,
But the Abbott of Burton ne'er tasted his
As long as his neighbour's lasted.'

This strange introduction to life on or below *terra firma* might have induced a claustrophobic condition into my young mind but, on the contrary, I have had an abiding interest ever since in cellars and their contents.

There followed the normal upbringing of a child from a middle-class provincial family: Burton Grammar School (founded in 1520), where I sat alongside the sons of brewers, maltsters, hop merchants and coopers. These were the trades of Burton, the Brewing Capital of Britain. The family business was printing and publishing the local newspapers. In 1937, I began to produce beer mats, manufacturing the first multi-coloured mat for Trumans Brewery, in six colours, to commemorate the Olympic Games. More of this in my chapter on beer mats.

In 1939, there was the Territorials and seven years Army Service and, after three years in the 8th Army, back to Britain to join Field Marshal Montgomery's No. 5 Public Relations Unit from D-Day to Berlin. I helped to launch *Soldier Magazine* throughout Europe until discharge, on my birthday in January 1946. I then went back to the family firm, founded by my Cornish forebears in the exodus around 1840, and so back to beer mats and an increasing interest in all things to do with 'Tavern Treasures'. I became the largest producer of beer mats in Great Britain.

Much later, when living near Newbury, Berkshire, I began to collect Victorian bric-a-brac and pub collectables and took a stall in Portobello Road market, in west London. I had two partners—a tea-planter and a TV script-writer—and on the window of our boutique we painted the title 'Queer Things'.—Liberace came by one day with his entourage and bought practically the whole stock! In 1968, a publican pal, who had been born in the Portobello Road, called in and we had a few jars in The Red Lion. 'Wish my pub was as packed as this on a Saturday morning' he said and, there and then, we conceived the idea of running the first pub antiques market. A few months later we opened the Royal Standard Antiques Market at Blackheath in south-east London. This incursion into market-trading brought me a wide range of contacts at the popular end of the antiques business and I specialised in those items which I really understood, i.e. 'pub' antiques. I collected old catalogues and price lists and explored trade museums both at home and abroad. I had friends on either side of the bar, who were mines of information about the Good Old Days and the old methods of storage, dispensing and display. So, over the years, I have accumulated quite a store of relics, books and illustrations of pub collectables.

The British pub, about which so much has been written, is unique and the envy of less fortunate countries. I have tried to define the almost mystical quality which gives our heritage its special appeal. First must surely come the Landlord—the 'Guv'nor'—and his team, for it is a personality business and he is always 'on stage' to inspire that special rapport between his customers and his staff. But after this the most important contribution comes from the décor—not just carpet and curtains but the paraphernalia, the knick-knacks, the trophies and memorabilia which represent years of collecting: the shining brass and copper, jugs and plaques, oil lamps and candlesticks, the polished beer pumps with porcelain handles, the inglenook with blazing fire, gleaming trivets, tongs and pokers. This book is intended to be both a reference and a guide to other sources of information. The extensive bibliography and lists of museums and societies will guide the reader to further areas of research. For the collector of the really unusual, however, there are no known references and this volume will, I hope, steer the enthusiast in the right direction to explore the fascinating world of bygone days in our great British pubs.

Charles E. Tresise
Greenwich 1982

1 The British Pub

This book has been compiled for those collectors who are interested in the British pub or tavern. The interpretation of the words 'tavern', 'inn' and 'bar' has varied with the years but we are concerned here with those splendid establishments which have catered for the needs of both travellers and 'locals' over the generations.

I use the term 'British' rather than 'English' pub because the pubs of Wales and Scotland and Northern Ireland have so improved in the last three decades that the following excerpt from the *Architectural Review* of October 1949 no longer applies:

> 'The word [it was then written] "English" is used here deliberately not by oversight, for the pub is primarily an English rather than a British institution and though it is to be found in other parts of the British Isles and even beyond, it is in England that it is most firmly rooted and that it reflects the drinking habits of the people.'

The pub, or its counterpart in any country, reflects the social habits of that land and you have only to consider the characteristics which you observe in, say, the USA, France or Germany to see that the British pub is quite different and reflects the special qualities of the British people.

The *taverna* was the precursor of our modern public house and dates back to the time of the Roman occupation and ale, now generally called beer, our national beverage, was certainly brewed by the Ancient Egyptians 5,000 years ago. The University of Pelusium was as famous for its breweries as for its scholarship and it is recorded that the students were neglecting their studies on account of the popularity of the numerous ale-houses. How times don't change! The tavernas offered accommodation and refreshment; wine was frequently served and sometimes entertainment was provided. Many had a chequer board painted onto the door lintel, to indicate that chess could be played, hence the frequency of 'The Chequers' as the name of a modern inn.

It was not until the Romans had departed and the northern Europeans had arrived, that ale became the national drink. The

Teutonic and Scandinavian influences established the drinking habits which remain to this day and much of the brewers' vocabulary is derived from these imported languages. The Danish word *öl* became 'ale' and cask sizes are still kilderkins, firkins, etc. For the Anglo-Saxons there were three kinds of establishments open to the public, the ale-house (*eala-hus*), the wine house (*win-hus*) and the inn (*cumen-hus*), and three kinds of ale, 'clear', 'mild' and 'welsh', and this choice remained for the best part of a thousand years.

In 1552, licensing laws were introduced and there is a clause in Magna Carta which lays down the measures by which ale was to be sold; earlier, in 1267, at the Assize of Bread and Ale, under Henry III, the price of these products was fixed. Weak ale was priced at a penny a gallon and better ale at a penny and a half.

In the mid-eighteenth century, public houses were advertised in the *Daily Courant* as 'Free from bondage of any particular brewer' and the true British pub has always been the product of individual landlords rather than large brewing chains. Nowadays the large conglomerates have taken over the brewing trade to a very great extent and there are comparatively few small breweries left. The modern pub often reflects the style adopted by brewers, who are more interested in creating profit than preserving history, but it happens, fortunately, that in many cases the two objectives coincide and there are many excellent houses, managed by brewers and multiple licensees, which have retained their traditional appearance. The true collectors' pub, however, is almost invariably one which has been privately owned or operated by a tenant-landlord as a free-house and it is from these pubs that the enthusiastic collector may be able to acquire the relics and artifacts of the past.

Collectors range from schoolboys who collect drip mats and book-match covers to international breweriana collectors who prize old corkscrews, seltzogenes and polyphons. Many items listed in the following pages can only be found in the cellars and attics of old pubs which have been in the same family for generations. Drink-trade artifacts now feature regularly in the sale catalogues of leading auction houses and the national and provincial press gives wide coverage to the boom in collecting, as do publications such as *Finders Keepers*, *Exchange and Mart* and *What's Brewing*.

Readers wishing to contact collectors in the USA would do well to liaise with the well-established breweriana clubs. Writing from the University of California at Los Angeles, where he is to be found at the Department of Economics, Professor George W. Hilton supplied the following information:

'The information on pub collecting is necessarily limited. As you are presumably aware, we don't have pubs as such. A few restaurants, typically steak and chop houses, attempt a pub decor. A few bars do so but it usually doesn't come off well. We do have two organisations of collectors of artifacts from American bars, breweries and liquor stores concerned with beer. The older is the Eastern Coast Breweriana Association, 30201 Royalview Drive, Willowick, OH 44094, founded in 1970. The younger is the National Association of Breweriana Advertising c/o Gordon B. Dean, Willson Memorial Drive, Chassell, MI 49916, founded in 1972. Obviously, this has not been an organised activity for very long. I belong to both, and edit the journal of the latter, *The Breweriana Collector*. This may bias me, but I confess a rather strong preference for the latter. The two organisations differ in that ECBA includes collectors of cans and bottles, whereas NABA restricts itself to beer-related artifacts excluding containers. NABA also seems to me the more intellectual of the two. I am trying to make *The Breweriana Collector* a popular journal of brewery history. ECBA is mainly organised for its annual summer week-end at an eastern brewery. ECBA is mainly eastern, and NABA is mainly mid-western, though both have members nationally.

In both organisations, collecting is mainly of trays, taps, markers, signs, glassware, coasters and labels. One member of NABA collects bricks from razed breweries, although how ne establishes authenticity I know not. I am the only member of either organisation who lists British breweriana as one of his collecting interests, though some other members collect it on a casual basis. I know two others in NABA who collect pump handle clips when in England. Our collecting is mainly of the old local brands which have been almost entirely superseded by national beers. The trend towards concentration in the industry has gone on for a century, but since World War 2 the pattern has changed from the majority of beer being brewed locally to almost all of it being brewed by a limited number of national firms. Current collecting is largely of the few remaining local brewers, who number under 30. Some members collect the national brands, of course. A member of NABA in El Paso literally attempts to collect an example of every issue of Anheuser-Busch advertising, encompassing glassware, trays, tap markers, point-of-purchase signs, and more. He must have a readily

A lovely sight for the supporters of the Society for Preservation of Beer from the Wood! Pretty Sarah Miles draws a foaming pint at a Campaign for Real Ale Festival.

expansible house for A-B produces some 48 million barrels of beer annually and spends over $100 million per year on advertising.

There are two men who operate mail auctions of beer-related artifacts, Herb Ashendorf, 21 Montclair Road, Yonkers, NY 10710, and William T. Hendricks Jr., 506, Remsen Street, Trenton, NJ 08610. The other principal markets are the annual conventions of the two organisations, plus an Antique Advertising show held thrice annually on the Indiana State Fair Grounds in Indianapolis. Several individual dealers specialise in beer artifacts. Mark and Lois Jacobs, 702 N. Wells Street, Chicago, IL 60610, have a shop which sells antiquarian items related to Chicago, sports, politics and the extinct local breweries, for example.'

In recent years, we in Britain have seen the revival of the so-called 'small brewer' and, thanks to the influence of the Society for the

Preservation of Beer from the Wood and the Campaign for Real Ale (CAMRA), a renewed demand for cask-conditioned beer. In earlier centuries, the brewing was generally done by the housewife. Indeed we still speak of the 'brewster' sessions, at which licences are granted, and 'brewster' is the feminine form of 'brewer'. In the Midlands until the mid-nineteenth century, the out-house of a large country house or farmhouse was generally referred to as the 'brewhouse' and 'brewery' is just the Frenchified version of the old Saxon word *brew-hus*. In those far-off days, before Women's Lib had been invented, the ladies of England enjoyed their freedom and from Thomas Platter, writing in *Travels in England* in 1599, we learn that:

> 'What is particularly curious is that the women as well as the men, in fact more often than they, will frequent the taverns and ale-houses for enjoyment. They count it a great honour to be taken there and given wine with sugar to drink; and if only one woman is invited, then she will bring three or four other women along and they will gaily toast each other; the husband afterwards thanks him who has given his wife such pleasure, for they deem it a great kindness.'

And so to collecting Tavern Treasures, the visible trappings which go so far towards the creation of just the right atmosphere—as Dr Johnson said in about 1800: 'There is nothing which has yet been contrived by man by which so much happiness has been produced as by a good tavern or inn.'

2 Behind the Bar

Bottles

Bottle collecting has been established as a hobby in Britain for a decade or more and, in the USA, for twice as long. The hobby now has its own magazines and price guides are published annually. One of the attractions of bottle collecting is that it only requires time and enthusiasm. Very little expense is involved in the first instance and there are bottle-collecting clubs throughout the country where advice can be sought and exchanges arranged. In the USA, it is the third largest collectable (after stamps and coins).

Glass as a container for beverages has a long history, of which the important dates are:

3000 BC   First glass containers made in Egypt, using sand cores.

300   BC   First blown bottles made in Egypt at Alexandria, but the art of blowing was lost after the decline of the Roman Empire.

AD 1200   Glass making revived in Venice, but not for beverage containers.

AD 1600   First English glass bottles made, using coal-fired furnaces.

AD 1663   'Sealed' bottles became fashionable.

AD 1695   England led the world with an annual production of over 3,000,000 bottles.

Important dates in the history of containers for specific beverages are:

Wine bottles

To 1600   Made in stone or leather (blackjacks).

1650   First glass wine decanters and bottles, sealed by oiled hemp wads and tapered corks.

1750   Cylindrical bottles appeared.

1802   Traditional shapes developed for burgundy, champagne and hock, and square for gin.

Beer Bottles
1872   Internal screw-stopped invented by H. Barret (UK).
1892   Crown Cork invented by W. Painter (USA).
1900   Automatic machines to fill and cap invented.

Mineral Waters
1685   Boyle published an idea for carbonating water.
1772   J. Priestley perfected the idea.
1813   Soda Syphon invented by S. Plinth.
1814   Egg-shaped Hamilton bottle invented.
1870   Flat-bottomed Hamilton gradually replaced the earlier shape and remained in production until the 1920s.
1872   Screw-thread bottle-necks invented.
1875   Codd's bottles, with marble stoppers, were invented and were in use until the 1930s.
1875   Swing stopper invented.

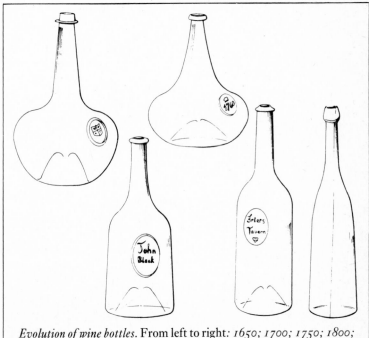

Evolution of wine bottles. From left to right: *1650; 1700; 1750; 1800; 1850.*

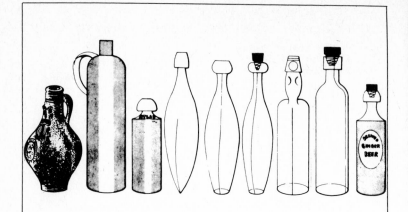

Evolution of beer bottles. From left to right: *1700; 1800; 1850; 1820's 3-piece mould bottle; 1872 internal screw 'blob-top' bottle; 1910 improved internal screw; modern beer bottle.*

Evolution of mineral water bottles. From left to right: *17th-century Bellamine Flemish ware jug; 18th-century English stoneware; 19th-century stone ginger beer bottle; the Hamilton bottle of the 1870s; flat-bottomed Hamilton with internal screw stopper made after 1872; Hiram Codd's glass marble bottle of 1875; 1890s' internal screw bottle with vertical sides; early 20th-century stone ginger beer bottle.*

Gordon Litherland, in his book *Bottle Collecting Price Guide*, makes several useful suggestions for categorising a beginners' collection. He suggests:

a) Bottles of the same category, e.g. beer, wine, minerals.
b) Commemoratives, such as those with Jubilee and Wedding labels.
c) Miniatures.
d) Examples showing evolution of one type of bottle, e.g. Codd's.
e) Bottles from one brewery, e.g. Bass.

The two most collected commemoratives are those produced for the Jubilee of Queen Elizabeth II and the marriage of HRH Prince Charles and Lady Diana Spencer. At the end of this book are The Brewers' Society lists of the Jubilee and Royal Wedding beers, all with splendid labels. One small independent brewery, Simpkiss's of Wednesbury, in the Black Country, only produced 5,000 Jubilee examples and each label was numbered and autographed by the Head Brewer. To make up a complete collection, one of these should be included, but they are difficult to find. Also listed are special brews for other occasions—all of which are collectors' items.

Among the most highly-prized commemorative bottles are those issued by Bass at Burton—Ratcliffe Ale (1869), the one-pint King's Ale (1902) and the Prince's Ale (1929)—the author remembers seeing the Prince of Wales drive through the town to start the brew on the latter occasion.

The commonest sources of supply of collectable bottles are old local rubbish tips. Research into local records will show where these tips were located and, although in many cases the land may have been reconstituted for development purposes, other areas remain untouched. River beds and canal bottoms also yield rare finds and there are literally hundreds of local collectors' fairs and bric-a-brac shops worth exploring. A study of the reference books available will quickly enable the collector to spot the unusual samples.

Miniatures

There are very few pubs which do not have at least a few miniature bottles of whisky, gin or cordials on display behind the bar. These are sold at railway station buffets and other places where people want to purchase just a large tot to take on their journey. The

Part of the collection of over 8,500 miniature bottles belonging to Mrs Ivy Grant.

collection of miniatures has become quite a popular hobby and there are a number of collections which run into thousands of different labels.

Mr David Maund has a collection of over 10,000 miniatures and

Mrs Ivy Grant of East Sussex has over 8,000 and the number is continually rising. There is now a Mini Bottle Club so collectors may establish liaison and arrange exchanges. This is organised by Mrs Paula Davis at her home in Uxbridge, Middlesex where she has a collection of over 3,000. It is in the USA, however, that home of Collectamania, that the largest collection, of nearly 30,000 different models, can be found. The author remembers, some thirty years ago, when he lived at East Lodge near Burton, being unexpectedly visited by a group of thirsty friends and, having a sadly-depleted cellar, decided to open his collection of about seventy miniatures. All these were put into a large punch bowl and topped up with soda to produce a remarkably palatable drink—very powerful too. Those early post-war miniatures would be worth a lot of money now!

An effective way of displaying miniatures, which also keeps them dust-free, is to use an old-fashioned corner cupboard—or a modern pine version. Three shelves can accommodate up to four hundred bottles and I have seen one cupboard in The Black Swan at Swanage, Dorset, with each shelf devoted to one category: whiskies, gins, liqueurs and so on.

Drinking Vessels, Ale Mullers, Flagons and Stirrup Cups

In Saxon days, the horns and drinking cups were made without a foot, so they had to be drained at a single draught, and it is these

A selection of Anglo-Saxon tumblers.

footless beakers that gave rise to the name 'tumblers', still currently in use. One of the earliest English drinking vessels was the blackjack, which was made of a single piece of leather, folded and sewn about six inches from the edges and then the outstanding strip beyond that stitched to make the handle and a separate piece sewn in to make the bottom of the vessel. The inside was treated with pitch for waterproofing and preservation. There is an old song 'The Leather Bottel' which reads:

'A leather bottel is good,
Far better than glass or wood,
And when the bottel at length grows old,
And will good liquor no longer hold,
Out of its sides you may make a clout,
To mend your shoes when they're worn out.'

It is said that returning French travellers reported that: 'the English men used to drink out of their bootes!'

Other names for old drinking vessels were: the bombard, after a piece of artillery in use at that time; the gaspin, which was about halfway in size between the large bombard and the blackjack; and the piggin, originally made from pig's skin. Shakespeare, in his play *Henry IV*, refers to Falstaff as that 'huge bombard of sack'. Some of these tankards held two quarts of liquor and, because they were tumblers, customers were inclined to drink the lot at one go. Indeed, King Edgar (tenth century) ordained that large vessels should have pins or nails set in them and that any person who drank past one of the marks at one draught should pay a fine of one penny. The vessels were designed to have eight sections, each marked with a peg driven into the wood on the inside and were known as pin or peg tankards. The famous Glastonbury tankard was made of oak and holds two quarts, divided into eight 'pegs'. It is from these peg tankards that we derive the expression 'to take him down a peg or two'. Indeed, in Scotland, they still speak of a 'peg' of whisky.

Pewter is the metal which one most readily associates with drinking in inns and taverns. This ancient metal, well known to the Romans, is a mixture of lead and tin with a touch of copper, and perhaps silver or antimony. Being cheaper to make than silver, it became very popular for the manufacture of drinking vessels and they were much more durable than when made in other materials. They were often made with lids, because the ale would frequently be warmed or mulled, and some of them had glass bottoms so that drinkers could see that the beverage was clear and not cloudy. These were introduced in about 1780, but modern versions abound, usually as sporting trophies and badged souvenirs. Some old flagons and tankards were fitted with lids, to enhance their price rather than for reasons of hygiene.

The tankard found in the ruins of Glastonbury Abbey.

The baluster shape, sometimes with a ball thumbpiece, was in common use from 1480 to 1830 but then gave way to the straight-sided patterns now used. Flagons came in 'straight-sided york' or 'acorn york', the latter having an acorn motif on the knob of the lid. After about 1770, lidded tankards lost their popularity.

Measures, as distinct from drinking vessels, generally had a brass or pewter rim around the top edge. This was to prevent an unscrupulous landlord from shortening the vessel!

Britannia metal was considered to be inferior to pewter, indeed it is known sometimes as 'poor man's silver'. It was invented by the Romans in Britain in AD 300–400 but then disappeared until the ecclesiastical revival in the eleventh century.

Imperial Measure legislation, introduced in 1826, accurately dates measures and tankards after that time and collectors can readily obtain this list. Pewter for drinking vessels is now frowned upon in pubs and, since the early 1930s, has been discouraged because of its lead content. In Great Britain, we have the exclusive

Pewterer's Society and, in the USA, the Pewter Collectors' Club; there is also a Pewter Club in Holland. An Act of 1503 required that all pewter be dated and marked, although the regulation was not universally observed, and good examples prior to that date remain, but are not 'touched' by the pewterer's mark. The Edinburgh pewter marks date from 1600 to 1760. There existed a great variety of such marks—various monarchs' initials, e.g. VR, WR, and also house marks of inns, e.g. the Saracen's Head or the Rose and Crown, or the inn-keeper's initials. This may well have been to identify any vessels which were stolen, in much the same way as modern pubs sometimes have their names sand-blasted onto the glasses—although I sometimes wonder if this identification does not make them all the more attractive to souvenir hunters! An Act of 1638 introduced standard measures for ale and wine and the Handbooks of the Inspectors of Weights and Measures list the stamp numbers relating to the county or town where the article was stamped. This is useful as a reference for collectors who wish to identify the place of origin of pewter vessels.

The decline of pewter came in the eighteenth century when glass manufacturers went into mass production. Pewter was comparatively expensive, because so many pewter mugs and tankards were stolen, as noted in a paragraph in *The Times* of 2 September 1796, which states: 'This day, the publicans in the Metropolis and its vicinity have come formally to an agreement among themselves, and withdrawn from the public the accommodation of finding them Pewter Pots, agreeable to a long established custom'. The publicans apparently collectively lost one hundred thousand pounds per annum, or so they claimed, in pots stolen. Plus ça change! Plus qui reste la meme!

There were very many different names for drinking vessels in the reign of King James I. Thomas Heywood, writing in 1635 in his book *Philocothonista or the Drunkard Opened, Dissected and Anatomised*, says:

'Of drinking cups divers and sundry sorts we have; some of elme, some of box, some of maple, some of holly etc. Mazers, broad-mouthed dishes, naggins, whiskins, piggins, creuzes, ale-bowles, wassel-bowles, court dishes, tankards, kannes, from a pottle to a pint, from a pint to a gill. Other bottles we have of leather, but they are mostly used amongst the shepherds and harvest people of the country; small jacks we have in many ale houses of the cities and

26

suburbs, tipt with silver: blackjacks and bombards at the court. . ..
We have besides cups made of horns of beastes, of cockernuts, of
goords, of the eggs of estriches: others made of the shells of divers
fishes. . .. Come to plate, every tavern can afford you flat bowles,
french bowles, prounet cups, beare bowles, beakers. . ..'

A noggin was a small mug made out of wood and is still used as a
measure for a quarter of a pint of liquor, whereas a pottle was a large
vessel holding two gallons.

Pewter and Britannia metal were, for generations, the common
material from which most drinking vessels were manufactured. In
the middle of the seventeenth century, Samuel Pepys talks of
'dining cabins' and of the provision of pewter on both household
and inn dining tables. A 'garnish of pewter' was the ambition of
every houseproud lady. These vessels would be displayed in the
dining room on a Welsh dresser, along with cruets for salt, pepper
and mustard. The spoons, too, were made of pewter.

Many different shapes and sizes of flagons were made and they
are fairly easily identified:

a) The acorn, an acorn-shaped flagon, dated from 1750.
b) The baluster measure, sixteenth to seventeenth century if
   English, or nineteenth century if Scottish, with a ball
   thumbpiece on the handle.
c) The beefeater flagon, 1660 to 1680, with a lid squashed like a
   beefeater's hat.
d) The bellied or bulbous measure, a very common shape in the
   Victorian period as a beer measure or in smaller sizes as a
   spirit measure and is still widely manufactured.
e) The portcullis, an Imperial measure from 1826 to 1830.
f) The society flagon or tankard, decorated with the emblems of
   the Friendly Societies and used at their meetings.
g) The larger sizes of tappit hen, with filling marks, or 'plonds',
   inserted to indicate the quarter or half-way measure.
h) The Art Nouveau period, 1890–1905, decorated with typical
   designs of the movement.

In Scotland, pewter was very expensive as tin was not mined
there and the best known measure was the tappit hen, fitted with lid
and thumbpiece and made in Scottish Imperial sizes, the Scottish
pint being equal to three Imperial pints (60 fl. oz). The chopin was
one and a half Imperial pints (30 fl. oz) and the mutchkin was three-

quarters of an Imperial pint (15 fl. oz). In Wales, pewter was virtually unknown. In Ireland, the haystack system of measuring was from one gallon down to half a noggin (a noggin being Irish for one gill). It had no handle and is now made in half pint to quarter noggin sizes.

Britannia metal, which looks so much like pewter, was first made in the mid-eighteenth century. Vickers' white metal appeared in 1769, consisting of 90% tin and 8% antimony, with traces of copper and bismuth. The metal is tin alloyed to antimony, whereas pewter is tin alloyed to lead or, in the earlier days, copper. Pewter is always cast, whereas Britannia metal is made in sheets (and marked EPBM after 1850). The surface designs are applied by a power press and only one seam appears. Handles and knobs are cast in pewter. Identification of Britannia metal objects is generally simple as they invariably bear the maker's name and catalogue number; collectors note that the number should not be mistaken for a date!

The Stirrup Cup was a drink offered to huntsmen at the Meet before setting-off for the day's hunting, and special cups became

Stirrup cups were usually fashioned in the form of fox masks, although hunting horns and hound masks are found occasionally.

fashionable about 1750. Many were fashioned to resemble fox's masks, hunting horns or hound's masks. As the hunting fraternity were generally well-to-do, the cups were often made with silver mounts, but they can also be found made in bone china and pottery. Best-known manufacturers were Derby, Rockingham and Whieldon—the latter's products being recognisable by the mottled colouring. Hall-marked silver cups are the most sought after and a silver fox mask made by Leader of the Field was sold a few years ago for £1,050, whereas an unmarked hound's head design fetched only £210. The best source of supply is in the hunting shires, in private collections or antique shops.

Ale mullers were used to warm up hot spiced drinks when required and were copper funnels without a handle and with no orifice at the pointed end. They were poked into the fire and Dickens, in *The Old Curiosity Shop*, describes the mulling of Mr Codlin's ale:

> 'The landlord retired to draw the beer and presently returning with it and applied himself to warm the same in a small tin vessel shaped funnel-wise for the convenience of sticking it far down in the fire and getting at the bright places.'

These ale mullers were also made in a shoe shape, usually of copper which had a high conductivity.

Punch Bowls, Wine Tasters and Accessories

It was under Queen Elizabeth I that the manufacture of glass was restarted in England after a period of decline. Elizabeth no doubt helped by imposing controls which prohibited the importation of foreign glass. Glasses for use in taverns were quite robust in order to reduce the risk of breakages and most of them had very short stems, if any stems at all. Some of them, known as firing glasses, were used at Masonic Lodges and had an especially thick base which could be used for hammering signals on the table in acknowledgement of a toast. One of the most popular shapes was the rummer and this is frequently found in manufacture today. It has a large bowl and a squat short stem and was originally used for punch.

The punch bowl was generally used on ceremonial occasions. This large vessel would be placed on the sideboard of the inn and the landlord would mix a punch to his own special recipe. The punch bowl is sometimes called a Monteith, after an eccentric eighteenth-century gentleman who had his coat cut with scalloped tails to resemble the design around its rim. The scalloped edge on a punch bowl was to accommodate the handles of the silver cups or glasses which hung around the side. Later punch bowls were made of china, often depicting naval scenes on their sides. Also supplied with punch bowls were wine tasters, or 'tastevins', which were small bowls of silver for tasting the brew, and nutmeg graters and ladles, also made of silver.

A porringer was for mixing porridge, as the name suggests, but it is sometimes confused with a bleeding bowl or a wine taster. When made in silver, with two handles like a loving cup, the wine taster or tastevin is still referred to as a porringer.

Various punch 'fillers' or 'lifters', were made to assist in the serving of the punch from the bowl into the drinking cups. There are many old recipes for punches using rum, brandy and curaçao, lemon, hot water, sugar, grated nutmeg, cloves and cinnamon. The great popularity of punch as a hot scented drink continued right up until the end of the nineteenth century.

Decanters and Wine Labels

In the eighteenth century, the wine or spirit decanter appeared at ceremonial wine- and spirit-drinking occasions and some of these early cut-glass examples are much prized amongst collectors. To indicate their contents, they would often have engraved gilt lettering with the word 'claret' or 'shrub', or whatever drink they contained. With the Georgian decanter, came the wine labels. These were made of silver or enamel and hung around the neck of the decanter on a fine chain. There is a collection of rare wine labels to be seen in the splendid wine museum of Harvey's of Bristol, the famous wine merchants.

Prior to the arrival of the printed label on wine bottles, it was customary to use parchment labels hung around the neck. These were known as bottle tickets. Curious names appear on those which have survived, such as 'Bounce', 'Nig', 'Mishianza', 'Bernis' and 'Hinogo'. No one now seems to know to what these exotic sounding names referred. Certainly they were of overseas and probably Far-Eastern origin. A traveller in those days would perhaps purchase some wine or spirits in a foreign land and ask for a label on which he could write the name, which could explain why one such label bears the name 'Zoobditty-match'!

Part of the collection of over 3,000 beer cans – one of the largest outside the USA—belonging to Paul Ley.

Beer Cans

Beer-can collecting is one of the newer hobbies to attract the attention of breweriana enthusiasts. It started in the USA just before World War 2 and Beer Can Collectors of America, formed in 1970, now has over 10,000 members and holds regular conventions on both a national and local level. The World Wide Beer Can Collectors (WWBCC) was formed to trade in collectable cans and became the largest such organisation in the world, although the leading commercial trader is based in Great Britain.

Early cans were made in a cone shape and closed by a crown cork, but were aesthetically unacceptable as they too closely resembled a tin of metal polish! The first British beer cans were introduced in 1936 by the medium-sized South Wales brewery, Felinfoel. In the same year, Simonds of Reading started canning and, in 1937, they marketed a Coronation brew in a cone-topped can bearing the Royal Crown; this has become one of the world's rarest cans.

Can production in Great Britain ceased from 1939 until 1949. From the 1950s onwards, the flat-topped can gradually replaced the cone shape, although the rip-off opener did not arrive until 1967. Around the late 1950s, the four- and seven-pint party can arrived and, for once, it was Great Britain that led the world in the development of a new form of pack.

The can collector looks for the most unusual and attractive surface design, as well as technical differences, such as tin-plate or aluminium, or cone or flat top. One such design, a set of seven James Bond girls, which appeared in the mid-1970s, now fetches $2,000 or more per set. As with beer bottles, commemorative cans are much prized, e.g. the World Cup series depicting finalist teams and those for the Queen's Jubilee, the Royal Wedding, and the Prince of Wales' Investiture. There are over 250 different cans in current use in Britain, including those used for soft drinks.

In Europe and Scandinavia, cans have not had the success that they have had here, except in Germany, where party cans are beautifully made and used extensively. Most countries pack their premium beers in cans for export and Sweden has produced some fine art-work. Australia and New Zealand both use cans widely and Malaysia packs its famous Tiger Beer in cans which sailors carry around the world.

Collecting cans is quite simple—you just have to have the time to find them and the money to buy them—and the thirst to drink the contents! They should be pierced twice at the bottom so that they look virginal when stood upright on a collector's shelf. If they are stored in a garage or out-house, they can be sprayed with a wax or vinyl aerosol to prevent rust.

Toby Jugs

Toby jugs are one of the most popular forms of pub decoration and have been manufactured since 1765 in a vast variety of different figures commemorating great personalities of their day. They were made to reproduce the well-known faces of admirals and generals, of actors and politicians, of criminals and, indeed, of anyone whose face became familiar to the public. Jugs moulded in the form of animals or figures are almost as old as the craft of pottery itself, but it is generally agreed that the first Toby jug was made by a Staffordshire potter, Ralph Wood, in 1765.

The name 'Toby' probably originates from Shakespeare's famous boozer, Sir Toby Belch, in *Twelfth Night*, although there

A selection of Toby jugs produced by Royal Doulton Potteries.

are other claimants. The achievement of sufficient fame to qualify for having a Toby jug designed after you came to some quite unusual and remarkable people. One of the earliest jugs is that of Martha Gunn of Brighton, who was a bathing woman (i.e. an operator of a bathing-machine from which people would take a dip) and she 'dipped' the Prince Regent on one of his first visits to Brighton. She died at the age of 88, in 1815, and always sported a Prince of Wales feather in her hat to commemorate that great day in her life. The jugs which were produced to commemorate her show her with a bottle of gin in her arms and this particular jug is often known as 'The Gin Woman jug'.

Another famous design associated with Regency Brighton is one known as 'Bluff King Hal', which purports to show Henry VIII but, in fact, the features are those of George IV, as he appeared at a fancy dress ball there. Some of the early designs are still being produced from the original patterns and they sell very well, particularly in the USA where they are considered to be a reflection of the character and conviviality of English pub life.

33

The earlier jugs were not only decorative, but also practical. In those days, beer in bottles had not yet arrived and beer pumps were at a very primitive stage of development and, therefore, the beer had to be carried from the cellar, or stillage at the back of the bar, in jugs for serving. The earliest jugs were all Staffordshire-made, but later the Rockingham Pottery at Swinton, Yorkshire, began to imitate the design, one of their most successful models being 'The Snuff Taker'.

Copeland Pottery began making Toby jugs in about 1829, after they had taken over the Spode factory and these can generally be recognised by the colour of the clothing, which is usually blue, with some yellow, and probably black shoes, whilst the face and hands of the figures are usually undecorated and remain in white clay.

As the popularity of collecting Toby jugs developed, the prices began to rise and, in 1918, an original Martha Gunn jug was sold at Christie's for what was then a record price of 66 guineas, and prices have been going up ever since. A set of jugs commemorating the war leaders of World War 1 or World War 2 would today fetch a very high price, although they were produced in enormous quantities at the time.

There are quite a number of pubs which display sets of Toby jugs, one of them being The Three Tuns at Blackheath in south-east London. An early imitator of Wood's original pattern was James Neal, who was Wedgwood's agent in London. He had a number of jugs stamped with the name Wedgwood, although that firm has never, in fact, included Toby jugs in its catalogue. Doulton entered the trade in 1815 at their Lambeth pottery in London and later produced a whole range of figures depicting characters from Shakespeare and Dickens. A popular series, known as portrait jugs, shows the likeness, albeit in caricature, of famous sportsmen, politicians and personalities of the world of entertainment.

Puzzle Jugs and Last-Drop Glasses

Puzzle jugs were produced up to the middle of the last century and were of very humorous style and design. They generally had tiny holes drilled just below the point where the drinker's mouth would contact the vessel, or below the spout, so that a guest when using it would find the liquor dribbling down his chin. A lot of these were made in Sunderland, in north-east England, and included a design whereby, on reaching the bottom of the glass, the drinker would see a large frog, cast into the pottery, lurking in the bottom!

These puzzle jugs usually carried an amusing rhyme along the side of the vessel, one of which reads:

'From Mother Earth I claim my birth,
I'm made a joke to man,
But now I'm here, fill'd with good beer
Come take me if you can.'

And another one:

'Here, gentlemen, come try your skill,
I'll hold a wager if you will,
That you don't drink this liquor all,
Without you spill or let some fall.'

Another design which is a collectors' item is what was called the 'Last-Drop glass'. When the drinker had swallowed what he believed to be the last of his ale, he would find engraved at the bottom of his glass a picture of a corpse hanging from a gibbet, so that even if he had turned the glass upside-down, he would not have drunk it to the last drop. This was the source of many a lost bet!

Hop Pots and Jugs

Hop pots and jugs come from a Sussex pottery on the borders of the famous Kentish hopfields where, from 1868 until fairly recently, it produced what is known as Rye Ware. This pottery was founded by a family called Mitchell and, in the middle of the last century, they experimented with glazes of greens, blues and purples for creating the traditional Sussex Ware, which had hitherto been brown. Hops have always been cultivated in the fields surrounding Rye, and through into Kent, and it was natural that the hop design, with its immediate association with bitter beer, should be used for the decoration of their wares.

Samples of the early hop pottery from the original Rye works can be seen in the museums at Hastings, Rye and Brighton and samples of the earlier jugs and vases are beginning to bring quite good prices. Yet, by prowling around the bric-a-brac shops, it is still possible to pick up these attractive items fairly cheaply.

3 Tools of the Trade

Beer Engines and Beer Pumps

'Not turning taps, but pulling pumps,
Gives barmaids splendid busts and rumps.'
(*New Statesman competition*)

There is no more pleasant sight to a beer-drinker than to walk into a bar and to see a glistening row of beer-engine handles lined up behind the bar for pulling up real ale from the cellars below; better still, if they are being pulled by a handsome barmaid!

For many centuries, beer was brewed on a more or less local basis and stored in oak casks made by the local cooper. The method of dispensing was very simple; there would be a cock or tap inserted into the side of the cask and the beer would simply be drawn off as required. However, as the road and canal systems improved and later the railways arrived, the problems of distributing beer over a wider area were overcome and the large brewing groups began to develop.

The need then arose for a more satisfactory method of dispensing the beer from the cellar up into the bar. Whereas, previously, the barrels of beer would be on a stillage, either in the cellar or behind the bar, it was now desirable for the beer to be kept cool in the cellar beneath and then pumped up for serving. It was in 1797 that Bramah invented what is believed to have been the first beer engine and this resembled the 'Accumulator' which had been invented earlier by Sir William Armstrong. The Bramah beer engine needed tubing to raise the beer and the inventor used old musket barrels for this purpose in his workshop in Soho, Birmingham. The first pewter tubes for raising beer appeared in 1860. In 1795, James T. Turner patented a beer engine and, in 1805, Thomas Wells, a cockfounder, also of Birmingham, produced the first beer cocks. It is interesting to note that, in the middle of the nineteenth century, there were at least thirty firms of cockfounders in Birmingham, all manufacturing a variety of taps for the beer and wine trades.

A cartoon by Cruickshank, in about 1830, shows beer pumps in use in a typical early Victorian gin palace. As will be seen from the illustrations accompanying this chapter, the early designs of beer engine were highly decorative and very ornate in appearance. Not many of these remain in use, although The Sussex Arms near the Pantiles, Tunbridge Wells, Kent, has a late 19th-century beer engine which has been connected to modern cylinders beneath the bar.

The Church Inn, Ludlow, Shropshire, has an 1895 solid brass beer-engine, with ornate lever action and porcelain handles, and is in perfect working order. The friendly proprietors of this family free-house serve a different 'visiting' real ale each week using this installation. Wadworth's from Devizes, Bass and Marston's from

An early Victorian barmaid.

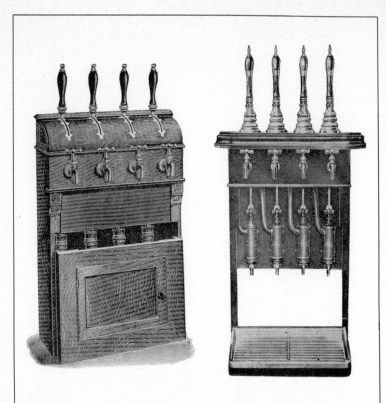

Examples of Beer Engines. From the 1934 catalogue of Harry Mason Ltd.

Burton, Buchan's from Bristol and Robinson's from Stockport are among the many cask-conditioned beers offered.

The beer-pump cylinder is known as the beer engine and there is now a move to replace the old brass engines with either glass or stainless steel cylinders, as it has been decided that brass is no longer an acceptable metal for the handling of beverages. This seems strange when one remembers that brass has been used for taps and cocks for both beer and other alcoholic drinks for many, many years with no apparent health hazard. This idea is certainly due to the move for standardisation in the Common Market countries and it is known that, in Germany particularly, the standards of control are much more rigid than in Britain.

In the early days of beer engines, the manufacturers used lead pipes to suppress the bacteriological action of the hops in the beer, a fact which was known to the Romans, who used lead in the manufacture of water pipes and containers for storing wine. The use of lead piping for beer engines went out between World War 1 and World War 2 and modern systems all use food-grade plastic tubing.

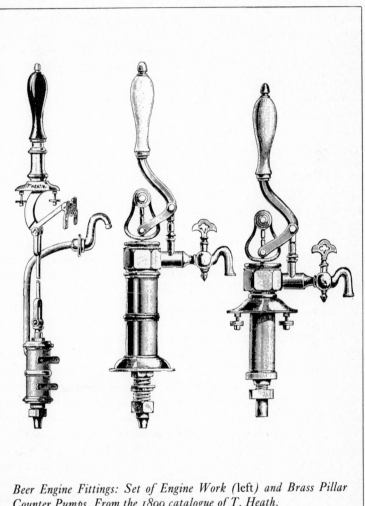

Beer Engine Fittings: Set of Engine Work (left) and Brass Pillar Counter Pumps. From the 1899 catalogue of T. Heath.

If a collector is so fortunate as to acquire one of these old beer-engines, it is not a difficult matter to convert the actual pump handle and cantilever to use with a modern under-bar cylinder. However, the cantilever which activates the pump varies in size from one model to another, so it is not always possible to adapt the equipment to get an exact half-pint pull which the normal engine would be expected to give. In fact, in pulling a pint from a beer engine, a good barmaid usually gives two full pulls, which should give an exact half pint each, but on the last pull she will serve just a bit less, so that the third pull, known as the 'topper', brings the measure up to the line at the top of the glass, which is the regulation mark required by the Weights and Measures Inspectors to ensure that the customer gets his full pint.

There was a protracted legal battle some years ago in order to establish that Guinness, with its distinctive head, could be sold in an overpint glass and that the head should not be considered part of the measured pint. Exceptionally this has now been agreed by the authorities and so the famous Guinness head has been retained.

In the 1950s, the brewing trade generally began to switch over to keg beers. The basic difference between keg beer and real ale is that keg beer is conditioned at the brewery and leaves the brewery in a sealed cask in which no further fermentation of the beer takes place. A sufficient pressure of CO_2 gas is used to force the beer up to the dispensing tap. Real ale, on the other hand, leaves the brewery in either a wooden or metal cask, but it has not been preconditioned and, when delivered to the public house, has to be racked and left to settle for forty-eight hours and then drawn for serving, either from a tap or a traditional beer pump, using suction to draw the beer up the pipe rather than gas pressure. In some cases, an electric pump is used to draw the beer from the cask to the bar and this is considered to be a perfectly acceptable way of serving beer by those purists who do not like to think that their beer has been forced up by gas pressure. Certainly the difference in taste is quite noticeable between the one type of beer and the other.

In recent years, the Campaign for Real Ale (CAMRA), has been very active in encouraging the brewers to retain, either wholly or partly, their production of traditional ales and this pressure group has had very considerable success in persuading the brewing trade to take action. CAMRA itself was preceded by the Society for the Preservation of Beer from the Wood, which still meets in Watling

Street, in the heart of the City of London, at a pub appropriately named Ye Olde Watling. They no longer insist on beer being drawn from the wood, since wooden casks have to a large extent been replaced by aluminium casks. However, there are still a few medium-sized breweries in this country which deliver their beer in oak.

Pump-Handle Clips

Collectors of paraphernalia connected with draught beer will find one of the more interesting items is the pump-handle clip. It is obviously desirable to identify the product coming from each of the row of pumps in the bar and the pump-handle clips, usually made of plastic, are fastened onto the handle and can form a fascinating collection. Some clips have been made in brass, wood or pewter. The beer-pump handles themselves are very collectable and, as they are generally mounted on a heavy brass base, they can be adapted to make attractive table lamps or door stops. With the revival of real ale, the manufacture of these pumps has increased enormously and a range of some thirty or more different porcelain handles is now available. The prize ones, from a collector's point of view, are the early Wedgwood and Doulton patterns, which date back to the early part of the century. One of the commonest of the older type of pump handle was the black ebonite model, shaped somewhat like a policeman's truncheon with two metal bands. It used to be an old trick to unscrew the top section and to challenge someone as to how much whisky one could get into the hollow handle. At first sight it appears large enough to take at least a double or treble shot of spirit but, in fact, it takes only a single whisky to fill it!

Barrel Tilters

Some of the most interesting relics of the draught-beer trade are what are known as 'barrel tilters'. In olden days, the drayman's job when delivering the beer was not only to unload it from his dray but to put the barrels up onto the stillage or wooden rack, in the cellar or behind the bar, and then to tilt them to the required angle so that the beer would settle fine and clear and ready for serving. As a hogshead (54 gallons) weighed about a quarter of a ton it was quite a hazardous job to handle these casks; so the ingenious Birmingham

Barrel Tilters from the 1899 catalogue of T. Heath. Top, from left to right:
the '*Acme' Barrel Tilter* – also known as the '*drayman's widow*'; the
Improved Tilt Rack; Screw Tilting Haunches. Bottom: *Improved Patent
Self-Acting Tilters.*

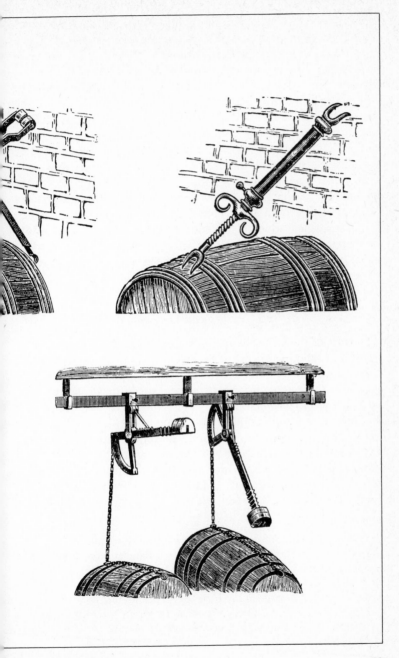

manufacturers invented a number of levers in order to assist him. The illustration (p. 42) shows the cleverest of these, which was known as a 'drayman's widow' because, if by chance the drayman should have an accident when handling one of these monster casks, his wife might well find herself in the parlous state of widowhood.

You can still find these drayman's widows in use in some of the wine cellars in France but, right in the heart of London, at The Cheshire Cheese in Fleet Street, two of them are still used everyday to handle the extra large casks in which the beer is delivered. The Cheshire Cheese serves over 2,000 gallons of beer every week and, as the cellar is not large enough to accommodate this quantity in 36-gallon barrels, the beer is delivered especially from Marston's brewery in Burton upon Trent in 54-gallon-capacity casks which are then stacked two high. Without the drayman's widow, it would be extremely difficult to get them all adjusted to exactly the right angle for dispensing. Needless to say, the beer is always pumped up by hand pumps, to the great delight of real-ale buffs.

Barrels, Bushes and Coopers' Tools

The craft of the cooper is the oldest of all the wood crafts—older even than wheelwrighting. The earliest containers were made of coopered wood, yet this old trade is now dying rapidly. In years gone by, there were dry coopers, who made pickle barrels, fish barrels and other containers which did not have to be absolutely leak-proof, and wet coopers, who made casks for liquids such as beer, wines, spirits and vinegars. All ships of the Royal Navy included a cooper amongst the crew to repair the casks, which contained everything from food and drink to gunpowder and shot!

In 1531, brewers were forbidden to make the barrels in which their ale was sold. The reason for that extraordinary prohibition is given in the quaint words of the preamble of the Act:

> 'Whereas the ale brewers and beer brewers of this realm of England have used, and daily do use, for their own singular lucre, profit and gain, to making in their own houses, their barrels, kilderkins and firkins of much less quantity than they ought to be, to great hurt, prejudice and damage of the King, liege, people, and contrary to divers Acts, Statutes, Ancient Laws and customs heretofore, made, had, and used, and to the destruction of the poor craft and mystery of coopers.'

head

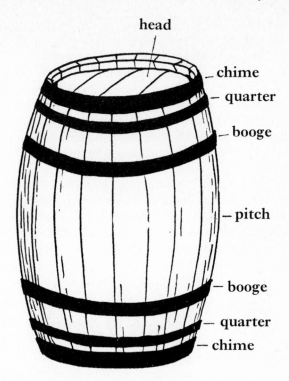

chime
quarter
booge
pitch
booge
quarter
chime

Diagram to show the hoops used in strengthening a cask.

The coopers were ordered to make every barrel which was intended to contain beer for sale in the capacity of 36 gallons. Ale barrels however were to contain only 32 gallons. (Ale was the stronger brew and was also sweeter than beer, which was hopped.)

As early as the sixteenth century, Derby had a great reputation for its ale. Sir Lionel Rash, a character in Green's *Tu Quoque, an Elizabethan comedy* says:

'I have sent my daughter this morning as far as Pimlico to fetch a draught of Derby ale that it may fetch a colour into her cheeks.'

It is interesting to speculate just how the brewers of Derby and nearby Burton upon Trent, managed to get their beer down to London in good condition.

Dorsetshire beers became famous and great quantities were shipped to London in the seventeenth and eighteenth centuries.

The excellence of Dorset beers was due to the peculiar qualities of the water of the area and Dorset ales are still highly regarded by connoisseurs throughout the south of England.

The tools used by coopers are unique to their trade and quite different from those used by conventional joiners and cabinet makers. They evolved over the centuries and, during his working life, a cooper would acquire three or four boxes of tools. It was usual for these to be raffled off at his death or retirement, or passed on to his son, should he be so fortunate as to be apprenticed to his father's trade.

In 1424, there were three hundred brewers in the City of London and regulations were enforced to ensure that casks held the correct measure. The coopers were ordered by the Lord Mayor, Richard Whittington, to mark with an iron brand all the casks made by them. A typical example of the cooper's mark with his name annexed is shown below:

By the turn of the century, the cooperage industry in the brewing trade was already showing signs of a slow decline, with the increasing popularity of bottled beers and the introduction of steam cooperage and various machines to shape the staves. All this meant fewer craftsmen, but it was the arrival of the metal cask, in about 1946, which quickly reduced the ranks of the journeymen coopers and few apprentices were indentured to the craft after that date. The remaining coopers were chiefly employed in repairing old casks or cutting down large casks to make smaller ones, rather than in the manufacture of new barrels. A good oak cask had a life of anything up to sixty years, so it will be seen that repairing barrels and fitting new staves remained an occupation in itself.

There are still a few working cooperages in England which are engaged in manufacturing barrels for the brewing, wine and spirit trades because there are still several brewers who pack their real ale in wood. The most important of these are: Bateman's, Burton-wood, Darley's, Hartleys', Jennings', John Willie Lees', Ridley's, St Austell's, Samuel Smith's, Theakston's, Wadworth's, and Young's.

The illustration of the Union Room, Burton upon Trent, shows a very large building, 375 feet in length and 105 feet in breadth, which held 1,124 'unions', or large casks, with a total capacity of 230,688 gallons. The union rooms of the brewery at the turn of the century contained about 4,500 unions, each with a capacity of 695 gallons. At that time, the brewery was processing 20,000 casks each week through its racking rooms.

The Union Room at the Bass Brewery, Burton upon Trent.

The only remaining example of the Burton union-brewing system is at the Bass brewery in Burton, although this was phased out of production in 1982, leaving only Marston's brewery, also at Burton, with a row of unions mainly used for yeast cultures.

Collectors who are looking for coopers' tools can refer to the Bibliography at the end of this book where the most important works of reference are listed. There is also an excellent establishment, called The Tool Shop, in Islington, London, at 288 Upper Street, where there is a fine collection of old woodworking tools, including some magnificent long planes, known in the trade as 'jointers', some of which are up to 6 feet long.

The names given to these ancient tools are quite fascinating, such as adzes, the bungflogger and the buzz, the chiv and the croze, the devil's tail and the dutchhand, the flagging iron and the flincher, the gorse and the jigger, the plucker and the topping plane.

Today, it is surprisingly difficult to find sets of coopers' tools when one considers the tens of thousands of coopers who were busy in cooperages, breweries and distilleries at the turn of the century. There were six hundred and thirty journeymen in one cooperage alone and Bass at Burton employed four hundred coopers just before 1900. Everyone of these craftsmen had his complete set of thirty or forty tools and one wonders where they have all got to. The most comprehensive illustrated list of coopers' tools is to be found in *The Cooper and His Trade*, by Kenneth Kilby. This book also lists all the casks made by both wet and dry coopers.

The great days of the cooperage industry were from around 1835 to 1914. The advent of the railway system enabled the brewers to deliver their products over much greater distances and the breweries were very closely associated with the development of the railroads. Indeed, the great house of Bass, at Burton upon Trent, originated in 1723, when a small carrier of goods by packhorse, whose name was Bass, sold his business to Pickfords, so that he could devote himself exclusively to brewing. Prior to that, he had been selling home-brewed beer prepared in his spare time, but the demand for the beverage grew to such an extent that he decided to go into the brewery business full-time.

The movement of beer over long distances meant that the casks received even rougher treatment than before and it was found that the barrel-stave which had the bung-hole in it, into which the beer was poured when filling, was the weakest point of the cask, so the firm of John Fearn of Sheffield, which later was to incorporate the Sheffield Cooperage, invented a two-part metal bush to reinforce the bung-hole. These were first made in about 1850, in cast iron, in the form of a male- and female-threaded washer, but it was soon found that iron was inclined to rust and contaminate the ale and, by

Coopers' tools and sundries from an early (c.1960) catalogue issued by John Fearn Ltd: a) Scotch Auger Bit with Screw Point; b) Belfast Crum Knife; c) Cylindrical Bung-Hole Borer for hand use; d) Nailing Adze; e) Buzz complete with Iron; f) Straight Drawing Knife; g) Chive complete with Iron; h) Round Shave of Scotch Pattern; i) Croze complete with either Hawksbill, English Patent, Scotch Patent or Saw Teeth; j) Flagging Iron, English Pattern; k) Bung Flogger with Cane Handle.

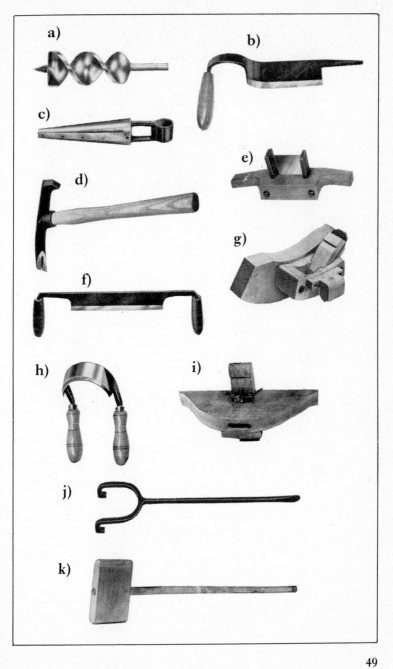

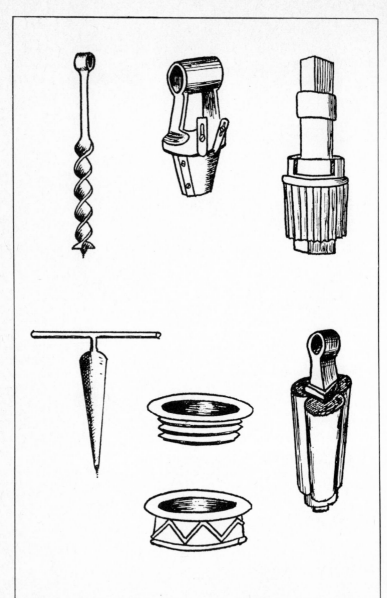

Tools used for inserting bushes into barrels. From left to right: *Auger; Flush Borer; Fluted Fixing Key; Tapered Auger; Screw Bush and Expanding Bush; Bush Expander.*

Brass barrel bushes were exported all over the world from 1880 onwards. They are still used by twelve brewers in Great Britain.

1880, a new design was developed, made of what is known in the trade as barrel bush metal. This is 77% copper, 20% tin and 3% zinc and lead. The nearest equivalent is gun metal. The particular qualities of this alloy are that it is hard enough to form the tapered thread which cuts into the oak of the barrel but malleable enough to stand the frequent hammering in of new bungs each time the cask is refilled. The tool for hammering is known as the bungflogger. These bushes were, and still are, cast with the name and the town of the brewer moulded into the die. This served to identify the brewer's property if several different brewers were supplying one pub, as in those days most of the outlets were free-houses.

The vast majority of these bushes were made by Fearn and most of them bear the engraved initials 'JF' as part of the die. The firm of Samuel Briggs of Burton made a few bushes around the 1920s and these bear the monogram 'SB'. Fearn still have about one hundred and seventy of the original dies and are still making bushes for those brewers mentioned earlier who are using wooden casks, but demand now is nothing compared with the quantities which were produced before the turn of the century. Many thousands were exported to Australia, New Zealand and the USA. Bass at Burton used to have 850,000 casks in circulation and each one of these would have been fitted with a bush. The storage of these casks at Burton occupied no less than 25 acres of ground. Guinness in Dublin regularly ordered them in 25,000 lots and Fearn were shipping them in thousands to the Far East, Australia and other colonies.

Barrel bushes can be mounted into match-strikers and ash trays. One hundred and ninety different brewery names are available to collectors.

The collector who wishes to start accumulating a range of bushes, will find them quite difficult to get hold of. Countless old casks were turned into water butts and can often be found behind the rows of terraced houses and country cottages. The bush is usually black with age and firmly embedded in the oak, and difficult to unscrew.

'Flag' is the name coopers use for the particular Norfolk river rush which is specially harvested for them. This is used for sealing joints in the casks, because the rush swells when it comes into contact with water or beer and seals any slightly open joint. When the bushes were screwed into the oak stave, the coopers would tie a piece of tarred yarn round the threads and this was wetted with linseed oil and helped to make a good seal. Another type of bush, patented by Oldham Brothers of Burton in the 1950s, was an expanding bush but, unfortunately, this was invented at a time when the use of wooden casks was rapidly declining and very few of these were ever put on the market.

An intending collector should seek out old cooperages which may be found in trade directories or pre-war telephone directories. They are nearly all closed down, but stacks of old casks can sometimes be found. Similarly, old brewery buildings, which are easily recognised by their tall water towers for gravity-feeding the liquor, usually incorporated a cooper's shop and, here again, old barrel staves and casks can sometimes be discovered.

The author was recently touring in Pembrokeshire and came across two old hogsheads in a pub garden in the Gwaun Valley and in each was a bush marked 'Worthington—Burton'. They were pre-1914 and, although black with age, in perfect condition. A few antique dealers have bushes on offer, but probably the best collection to be seen is that belonging to the author and the one at the excellent Bass Museum at Burton upon Trent. Barrel bushes polish up to a beautiful soft golden glow and make an excellent display on old oak beams or mounted onto beer-barrel ends.

The 'beaver' was a small barrel used by farm workers in earlier days to carry their day's ration of beer to the fields. These also make very collectable items as they are small enough to display in the house and are often beautifully made, sometimes bearing the initials or name of the owner.

Funnels and Beer Filters

The gleaming copper funnels still used in the cellars of any pub serving real ale make a very attractive collection and come in a whole variety of sizes. There are funnels in enamel and tinplate, although most are in copper, and there are cellar funnels in special shapes for pouring the ullage, or waste beer, into the various forms of filter used for clarifying the drip from the tray underneath the beer pumps in the bar. These filters were fitted either with a sponge or a sieve to retain any foreign matter that might have got into the ullage. There were also canvas beer filters into which the beer would be poured and seamless felt filter bags. Another filter for cleansing wine, oils and cordials used either canvas filter bags or filter papers or a combination of both. Copper filters, currently known as the 'Friar', were produced under a variety of names, including the 'Sun', 'Sparkle', 'Quartain', 'Barnsbury', and 'Thornhill'; all were similar in appearance and operation. They are frequently to be seen polished and decorating the older type of pub, where they make attractive containers for flower arrangements.

Measures and 'Optics'

'A just measure is a joy unto the Lord but a false measure is an abomination in his sight.'
(Proverbs. Text carved over the entrance to the Fruit and Vegetable Market in Greenwich.)

Legislation concerning the amount of beer sold to the public in Britain dates back to Magna Carta. Governments ever since have been concerned in ensuring that the public receives a just quantity for the money which it pays and the collection of the different types of measures is a fascinating hobby.

The earliest measures were made in pewter and many Acts of the Authorities and Parliament attempted to control the dispensing of beer, spirits and wine. Prior to the middle of the nineteenth century, the only method of controlling the measure was to have a line on the vessel concerned or to make a vessel of exact capacity and stamp the quantity on the outside. It was in about the middle of the nineteenth century that the Birmingham inventors turned their attention to producing a simpler method of pouring out spirits, which were rapidly coming into vogue in the public houses.

The earliest forms of spirit measures can be seen in the old trade catalogues from about 1860 onwards and some were most ingenious in their design. The modern spirit measures first appeared in the trade catalogues from about 1870 onwards. The best known of these was that invented by Gaskell & Chambers at Dale End, Birmingham, and registered under the trade mark 'Optic'. The first model was called the 'Optic Pearl' and this was in use until after World War 2. At about that time, the optic of modern appearance came in and these are now pretty ubiquitous throughout the bars of Britain. Their use has also spread into some parts of the USA and certainly into France. A number of other manufacturers have produced devices of similar appearance.

It was in 1963 that legislation was introduced requiring that optics should be tested and Government-stamped and this applied to the original 'Pearl' optic. The modern spirit measure also has to be sealed. This prevents the licensee or barman from cleaning them effectively so that, every time they require any attention, the seal has to be broken and the unit cleaned, rebuilt and then resealed, for which, of course, the Weights and Measures Department charge a fee. When the seal is attached, it is dated so that collectors can readily see when a measure was last tested and gain some idea of its age. Some of the earlier 'Pearl' optics are still to be found, although they are becoming increasingly rare and, if they do not have a seal on them, then it is pretty fair to assume that they are pre-1966.

Around 1900 there appeared the first of many devices to accurately pour fixed measures of spirits from the increasingly popular bottles. Hitherto spirits had been served from glass or porcelain jars, using a 'tot' measure, but the continuing rise in the tax on potable liquors called for more accurate control. In the 1899 catalogue of T. Heath, there appears the 'Improved Tilting Measure', which dispensed capacities of 3, 4, 5 and $5\frac{1}{2}$ 'out' of a gill. By 1914, the same firm, now called W.H. Heath Ltd, were offering the 'Opal-de-Luxe' range of measures and these were stamped by the Board of Trade to certify their accuracy. The Harry Mason Ltd (Birmingham) catalogue of 1934 offers a wide range of their 'Visible Standard Tap' in sizes of $\frac{1}{18}$, $\frac{1}{20}$, $\frac{1}{22}$ and $\frac{1}{24}$ of a pint with a whole selection of brackets and stands to display them.

The modern 'Optic' measure (Gaskell & Chambers) became popular after World War 2 and the original 'Pearl' optics made by them at Dale End, Birmingham, are now prized collectors' pieces. There are still a few pubs using these but, as it is difficult to adjust them to give the accuracy required by the Trading Standards offices, they are generally relegated to use in private bars.

The regulations require that potable spirits, i.e. whisky, gin, rum and vodka, shall be served in a stamped measure of $\frac{1}{3}$, $\frac{1}{4}$, $\frac{1}{5}$ or $\frac{1}{6}$ of a gill. The $\frac{1}{6}$ measure is almost universally used in England, but in Scotland the $\frac{1}{5}$ size has been largely used and occasionally one comes across a 'four-out' pub (i.e. a pub that sells spirits in $\frac{1}{4}$ of a gill quantities).

In 1877, we hear of the 'Holborn Champagne Tap', Registered No. 307655. This was for use when it was required to draw off a glass of champagne, perhaps for an invalid, without losing all the pressure in the bottle. The corkscrew incorporated in the tap had a hollow stem.

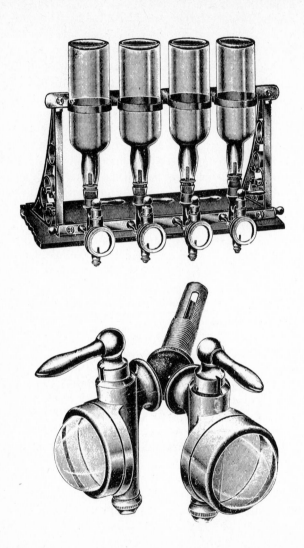

Measuring Taps from the 1926 catalogue of Gaskell & Chambers Ltd:
*'Optic Pearl' Measuring Taps with nickel-plated scroll bracket (*top
left*); 'Optic Pearl' Measuring Taps with double connection to draw
different sized measures from one spirit urn or cask (*top right*); 'Optic
Pearl' Measuring Tap for peg-tap glass urns, with double connection*

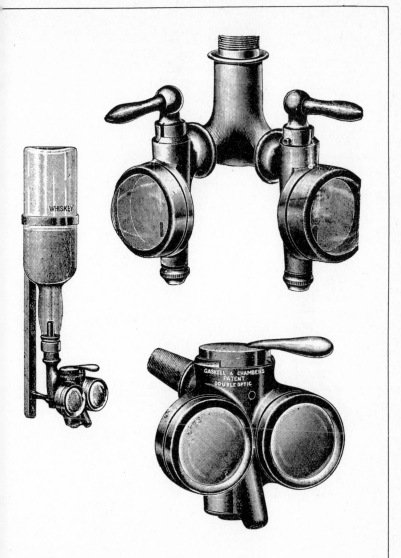

*(*bottom left*); Patent 'Double Optic' Measuring Tap – this tap has a
double action, one measure fills while the other empties – made for
bottles, barrels and kegs (*centre*); 'Double Optic' Measuring Tap
(*bottom right*).

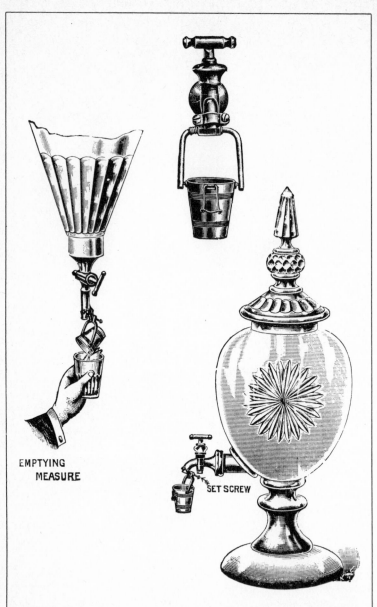

EMPTYING
MEASURE

SET SCREW

The 'Improved Tilting Measure'. From the 1899 catalogue of T. Heath.

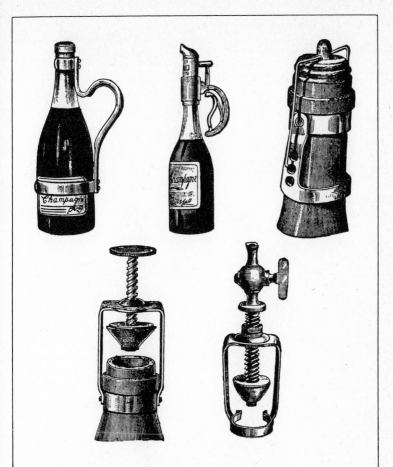

Champagne Stoppers and Taps from the 1899 catalogue of T. Heath.
From left to right: *Champagne Bottle Holder; Patent Champagne*
Tap; Bottle Stopper; Screw Bottle Stopper; Screw Bottle Stopper
with Tap.

Spirit Jars

In late-Victorian days, the serving of spirits and wines was
generally by ordinary tap or spigot directly from spirit jars. These
are highly collectable and expensive items to buy, but some of them
are extremely attractive in appearance as the next pages show.
They were made in pottery with various transferred illustrations, or

From the 1899 catalogue of T. Heath. From left to right: Porcelain Spirit Caskets; Porcelain Spirit Vase; Special Whisky Urn in Cut Crystal, fitted in polished copper and lacquered brass or in best nickel-plated stand; Special Double Urn Standard fitted with either 1-gallon or 2-gallon urns.

From the 1899 catalogue of T. Heath. From left to right: *Special Triple Ornamental Urn Standard; Porcelain Spirit Barrels; Crystal Cut-Glass Special Spirit Urns.*

in engraved glass, and were fitted with a brass tap. The capacity of these spirit jars was from one to three or more gallons and they were regularly topped up from the barrels of spirits, which were either kept in a room above or high on a shelf over the bar.

Alternatively, the barrels of spirits were kept in the cellar and brought up by a hand-operated spirit pump. A fine example of the storage of spirits on a gallery behind the bar can be seen in Heneky's pub in High Holborn, London, which must be one of the finest and best preserved examples of a typical nineteenth-century London tavern. The copper tubes down which the spirits descended are still in place.

Corkscrews

'Bottlescrews', or corkscrews as we now call them, first appeared in the early eighteenth century. The late André Simon, in *Bottlescrew Days*, quotes from an anonymous English poem, printed in 1770, which describes a dream about a dinner party at which the host eventually has to break off the neck of a bottle of wine because he cannot withdraw the recalcitrant cork; he first tries with his teeth and finally pushes the cork into the bottle, at the same time getting his thumb jammed into the neck! In the dream, Bacchus appears and:

> 'He sate majestick 'cross his tun
> And said: "Hail! dearest Rev'rend Son
> Whose bulky paunch and rosy face
> Proclaim thee of the toping race.
>
> Last night (for we above you know
> See all things that are done below)
> I saw thy conscious shame and grief
> And come to minister relief.
> For lo! this crooked instrument
> All future mischief shall prevent.'

Bacchus then produces a 'bottle-scrue', so the dreamer sets to work to make a similar device and:

> 'Now to the mighty task he sets
> His hands and o'er the anvil sweats
> First puts the iron in the fire
> And hammers out the glowing wire

Then tortures it in curls around
As tendrils on the vine are found
Sharpens the bottom round the top
And finished bears it from the shop
Well pleased a Bottle-scrue he names
And Sacred to the god proclaim.

This curious engine says the priest
Shall strech my fame from West to East
Me, the fox hunting tipling Squire
And cunning Curate shall admire.
Me, shall the raking Templar praise
And altars to my glory raise
When privately he treats his whore
And this famed scrue secures the door.
By me shall Bermingham become
In future days more fam'd than Rome,
Shall owe to me her reputation
And serve with Bottle scrue the nation.'

Well, Birmingham certainly became the 'Corkscrew Capital of the World' (American catalogue description) and, in the nineteenth century, dozens of patents and registrations for corkscrew designs were taken out in that city.

Early glass bottles were stoppered with wooden wedges or plugs of oiled hemp, or Spanish cork dipped in pitch, to achieve an air-tight seal. An awl or dagger was used to remove them. As it became more common to supply wines in bottles, it became necessary to develop a stopper which would discourage unscrupulous merchants (and butlers) from adulterating the contents. An Act of Parliament in 1728 prohibited the importations of wine in 'flasks, bottles or small casks'. This was designed to prevent smuggling but the Act was repealed in 1802, after which the modern-shaped wine bottles rapidly gained popularity. This heralded the Golden Age of Corkscrews.

In 1881, a book was published in Birmingham, (an edition of only fifty copies for private circulation) entitled *Birmingham Inventors and Inventions* by R.B. Prosser, the retired Head of HM Patent Office. He records all patents registered in Birmingham from 1722 to 1852, when the Patent Law Amendment Act came into force, during which time inventors could simply register their designs instead of going through the much more expensive and time-consuming business of taking out a patent. Many designs were thus put onto the market without the protection which a patent gives. The following list records some of the most interesting designs from the Victorian age.

Some Patents Granted for Designs of Corkscrew

1795 Samuel Henshall in Birmingham improved on the patented 'King's Screw' with a double thread and double-action housed in a brass cylinder and often incorporating a brush housed in the handle.

1802 May 7, Patent No. 2617, by Edward Thomason, later Sir Edward. Known as the 'Ne-plus-ultra' design, this consisted of two concentric screws, one left-handed and the other right-handed, the latter being hollow to allow the other to work within it. This was known as an hermaphrodite thread.

    When the worm had penetrated to the proper depth, the second screw came into operation, the handle still being turned in the same direction and the cork being literally screwed out of the bottle by a steady pull directly in line with the axis of the bottle. Then, by turning the handle in the opposite direction, the cork was discharged without the fingers being soiled by touching it. It had previously been the custom for wines to be decanted in the cellar or butler's pantry, with the possible risk of adulteration!

    This was made under licence by Messrs Heeley, Barlow, Robert Jones and Dowler and collectors will find these names stamped onto the metal.

1839 July 2, Patent No. 8139. Charles Osborne patented a corkscrew incorporating coiled springs.

1840 Job Cutler, described as 'Gentleman' and Thomas Gregory, Machinist, patented a device for cutting corks and forming necks of bottles.

1840 October 8. Robert Jones and Sons, Birmingham, registered the design of a corkscrew with two spikes to prevent the cork from turning.

1843 Alexander Southwood Stocker patented a stoppering bottle and corkscrew.

1844 May 7, Loach's Patent Application No. 10.176 for a corkscrew with brush.

1847 Drays' registered an improvement to the 'King's Screw' pattern with brass barrel and double screw and ratchet handle.

1855 William Lund patented two designs known as the 'London Rack' and the 'Lund's Lever'. The latter consisted of an ingenious lever action which fitted round the collar of the bottle. A separate helix-thread corkscrew penetrated the cork and hooked on to the lever, enabling the cork to be withdrawn by assisted lever action.

These were manufactured under licence by Messrs Weiss, Evans, Hooker, Retton, Mapplebeck & Lowe, Lowcock and Samuel Cotterill. Lund also registered a pocket corkscrew with the worm enclosed in the hollow handle for safe transportation, but which fitted together so that the case formed a 'T' handle when in use.

1864 Charles Hull patented the 'Royal Club' corkscrew with a single side-lever and arm.

1870 William Rockwell Clough, in the USA, invented a machine for drawing twisted wire threads. Hitherto, the worm had a helix-thread which presented a flat surface to the cork giving a better cutting edge. The twisted wire was cheaper to produce but more likely to damage the cork.

1873 Edward Wolverston registered the 'Tangent Lever' action which was made by Heeley of Birmingham and sold for 20/- a dozen.

1874 John Burgess and Albert Fenton patented a brass lever corkscrew with an ingenious side-lever action.

1876 Patent No. 297.635. Wolversons—The 'Signet'.

1880 Bakers 'Lever Corkscrew' patented and manufactured by Heeley. Heeley later took over the patent.

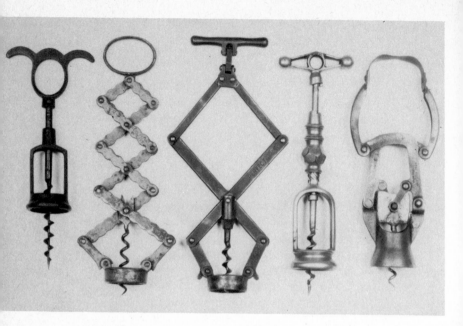

From left to right: *Steel corkscrew with diamond date code '14th January 1876'; an unusual example of Weir's Patent No. 4377 concertina lever corkscrew also marked 'J.H.S.' and 'B'; the 'Perfect' French concertina lever corkscrew; a 'Diamant' continuous action corkscrew by J.H. Perille of Paris; an unusual French lever corkscrew 'The Butler'.*

1880   Bar corkscrews of heavy brass and steel construction, were invented at about this period. They were clamped or screwed to the bar counter and incorporated quite complicated lever actions designed for speed in action. Bottled beers, and especially Guinness, were stoppered, often on the premises, by corking, so a rapid action corkscrew was required.

     The 'Safety' was a model in typical Victorian decorative style, but very efficient. Original models are still in use today and one such can be seen in action at The York Minster, now re-named The French House, in Dean Street, Soho, London. This pub has been in the Birlemont family for two generations and the present incumbent, M.

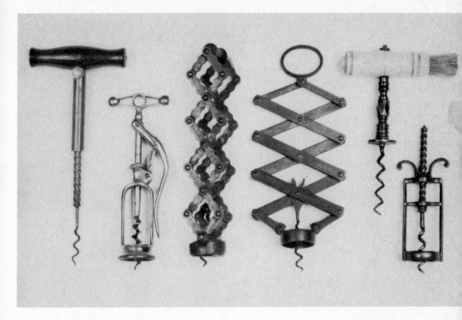

From left to right: *a rare direct-pressure corkscrew similar to Hull's 'Presto';
J.H. Perille's patent single side-lever corkscrew 'Le Presto'; a rare example of
Weir's 'Double Concertina' corkscrew, Patent No. 4283, also marked
'J.H.S.' and 'B', with two sets of hinged levers; Weir's 'Concertina'
corkscrew, Patent No. 12804 of 1884 – usual version; a fine simple
corkscrew with bone handle and brush, turned steel shank, fluted flange and
angled helix screw; an unusual steel corkscrew, probably 18th-century.*

Gaston, reckons that his Safety model has already drawn
over half-a-million corks, and it is still as good as new.

Other bar models were the 'Merritt', 'Don', 'Acme',
'Shamrock', 'Eclipse', 'Crown Cork Opener', and
'Unique'.

1884 September 25. Mr Weir patented and James Heeley
manufactured a 'Concertina' action corkscrew. This was
an eight-lever action, sometimes known as a 'lazy tongs',
which multiplied the pull exerted by means of a system of
scissor-type levers, so enabling the most recalcitrant cork

Gaston Birlemont, proprietor of The French House in London's Soho, demonstrates an original 'Safety' corkdrawer, which has been in use since 1900 and has extracted over half a million corks.

70

to be removed with the minimum of effort. This device was described by James Watt, the most famous inventor of his era, as 'the cleverest mechanical device that I have seen from this prolific inventor'. It has recently been adopted by The Guild of Sommeliers as their recommended hand corkscrew and is now in production, as a replica, in Birmingham.

1885 Goodhall patented the 'Holborn Lever Action', now a rare collector's item.

1888 James Heeley and Sons invented a twin side-lever action model.

1890 Ladies' corkscrews became popular, with silver or ivory handles to open scent jars, often part of a fitted travelling case.

1902 A.D. Armstrong's 'Irresistible' and 'Pullezi' marketed and manufactured by Heeley.

The first recorded sale of a corkscrew is a receipt for three shillings and sixpence, in 1686, to a Dr Claver Morris. By 1799, Birmingham had registered ninety patents and Manchester twenty-seven, and by 1819, Birmingham had one hundred and eighty-seven against Manchester's sixty-three.

Sir Edward Thomason in his *Memoirs* writes:

'I now turn my attention to the improvement of the corkscrew. At this period (1801) it was a kind of fashion for persons to draw the corks of the wine even at their own table and which not only required some strength and skill but was sometimes attended with accident by the breaking of the neck of the bottle and furthermore it was next to an impossibility to take the cork from the worm without soiling the fingers. To avert these two inconveniences, I directed my improvements and I produced a combination of the three screws working together, and following each other, so that on piercing the cork with the point of the worm, and continuing to turn the handle, the cork was drawn out, and by turning the handle the contrary way, the cork was discharged from the worm.

I obtained His Majesty's Royal Letters Patent for this invention under the name of 'the Ne-plus-ultra' corkscrew. I enjoyed the privilege in the manufacture and sale of these for a term of fourteen years. The patent answered well, and it not only made my name

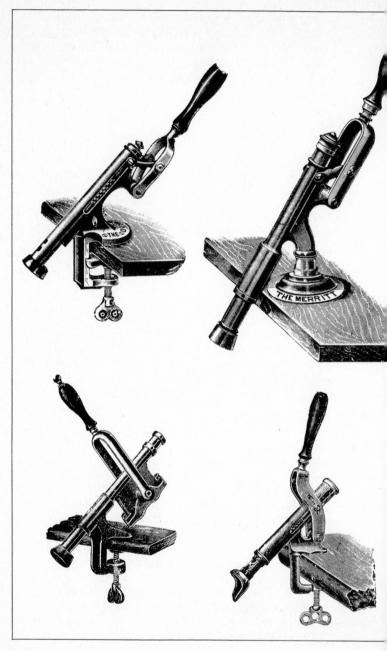

Bar-Mounted Corkdrawers from the 1926 catalogue of Gaskell & Chambers Ltd. From left to right: *the 'Don'; the 'Merritt'; the Rotary 'Eclipse'; the 'Swift' or 'Shamrock'; the 'Acme'; the 'A1'; the 'Unique'; the Original 'Safety'.*

known as the inventor but was the means of introducing other articles made in my manufactury, as fine buttons, jewellery and steelwork. It appears that I made during the fourteen years about a hundred and thirty thousand and a larger number have been annually called for, owing to the very great reduction in the price. In 1801, the shopkeepers in London sold them at one guinea each, but in the course of ten years, they were sold at the low price of four shillings which meant that the price was in the reach of all classes.

The Earl of Mountnorris (then Lord Valentia) on returning home from his celebrated travels in India, was so kind as to relate to me an anecdote which occurred at some small city on the borders of the Red Sea during his short stay there for refreshment. He heard the native servant call out "Bring me the Thomason". His lordship enquired if a person of that name was there and was answered, "The man was only asking for the machine to draw the cork".

Thus do the Birmingham manufacturers find their way to the remotest corners of the globe. Mr James Watt, the celebrated engineer, paid me a high compliment for this novel mode of applying the three screws.'

Mid-19th-century corkscrew, with handle and open frame, each formed by a pair of bronze putti, with Archimedean screw.

The same Sir Edward Thomason was one of the most prolific inventors in Birmingham for very many years and his memoirs make fascinating reading.

Advertisers began to use corkscrews for promoting patent medicines and cosmetics and wine merchants and distillers to advertise their products. There were usually cheap wire-thread models of no great intrinsic value but are sought after by collectors for the famous names which some of them carry.

After the end of this period, corks were extensively used by apothecaries and perfumers for sealing medicine and scent bottles and, as the necks of the bottles were somewhat inconsistent in width, they usually had a cork press behind the dispensing counter. These consisted of a pair of levers, which exerted pressure on a series of serrated holes of various sizes, enabling the chemist to compress a cork so that it would fit and seal the bottles. These late Victorian levers are rarely seen now, but occasionally one can be found adapted for use as a door knocker on an old-established pharmacy door.

Examples of Cork Presses. From the 1899 catalogue of T. Heath.

75

Collectors of corkscrews will be aware that the leading auction houses regularly feature sales of corkscrews in association with the wine auctions. The best source of supply is the kitchen drawer of any old house that has been in the family for a few generations. Entry (other than by burglary) is quite a problem, but at auctions there is often included an item of 'sundry kitchen ware', or some similar category, and old kitchen implements are included.

A rare curiosity for the collectors is the left-handed corkscrew! Oh yes! They DO exist. An old friend of the author, who was manufacturing many of the articles described in this book as far back as 1920, tells of the fun they used to have by handing a guest a 'left-hander' and paying him the compliment of asking him to draw the cork for the after-dinner port. He would self-consciously handle the bottle with great care and then, screw as he might, the corkscrew just would not penetrate, to his great embarrassment!

Kendal Graves, for that was his name, also gave a good tip on how to extract, from a bottle of wine, a cork that had, due to its softness, disappeared into the bottle instead of coming out with the screw. By dropping a loop of string into the neck of the bottle, it is possible, with a little ingenuity, to hook the loop around the cork and to pull it out. The thickness of the string allows air to enter the bottle, thus reducing the internal suction which would otherwise make the operation difficult. On the other hand, you can still buy a cork extractor, consisting of two or three wires with 'L'-hooked ends which do the same job. Several variations were catalogued in 1899.

Finally, there is a method of de-corking bottles which does not require a corkscrew at all! When corkscrews were just coming into popular use, it was the fashion to remove completely the neck of the bottle by using 'cracking pliers', now called 'port tongs'. These can still be found in antique shops, but frequently the vendor is unaware of their real purpose. These pliers are heated in the fire and then clipped round the bottle-neck, just below the cork; after a few seconds a cold, wet towel is wrapped round, and 'hey presto!', with a clunk-click, the neck of the bottle is broken away cleanly. This is particularly suitable for vintage wines, ports and so on, as there is no disturbance whatever to the contents.

Collectors who wish to study current trends in corkscrew design should study two American research reports. The Wine Institute of San Francisco, California, published a very detailed paper in the

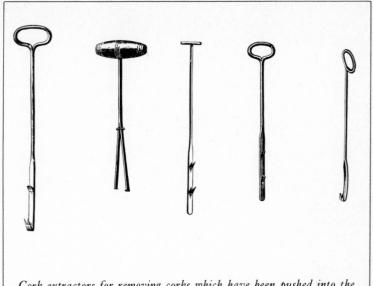

Cork extractors for removing corks which have been pushed into the body of the container. For use in jars, quarts or pints, or bottles. From an early (c.1920) catalogue of Barthes-Roberts Ltd.

May 1946 issue of the *USA Wine Review*. They went to immense trouble to take X-ray photographs of the action of the worm, or helix, as it penetrated the interior of the cork so that the best possible design could be adopted. In 1977, Messrs Kraus and Babbidge produced their report, amusingly entitled *Symptoms of Withdrawal*.

The Archives of the Birmingham City Library also contain many of the original patent applications and design drawings.

Wine Case Ends

The rapidly increasing number of wine bars appearing up and down the country has led to an interest in collecting items connected with the packing and presentation of wine and one very attractive such item is the case ends in which bottled wine is shipped from abroad. These are usually stamped with the name and style of the particular shipper or chateau and some of them have quite attractive line drawings of the establishment burnt into the wood by what used to be called pokerwork, but is now known as pyrography. When polished up, these make an attractive form of decoration, either for wine bars or for the enthusiast's own study or home drinking corner. Bin-end labels and wine-bottle labels are also collectable items.

Seltzogenes or Soda Syphons

Seltzogenes, or soda syphons, were invented by Charles Plinth in 1813 and were mainly used for home drinking and not often seen in pubs until 1880.

A catalogue produced by the British Syphon Manufacturing Company, in about 1905, illustrates the range of Seltzogenes, as they were then known, produced by that company. Successors to the same firm, British Syphon Products (Coldflow) Ltd, of Eastbourne, Sussex, are now the largest manufacturers of soda syphons in Great Britain, although the earlier models, with their attractive lattice-work covers, went out of production in about 1930. The illustrations show various models and, as they were produced in very large quantities from 1900 onwards, they are still to be found in bric-a-brac and collectors' shops. Indeed many of the models dating back sixty or seventy years are in perfectly good working order.

The earlier models were activated by packets of what were referred to as 'English acid in small crystals and bicarbonate of soda special prepared' and, with various flavourings, these produced soda-water or seltzer water, potash water or lithia water, as well as lemonade and sparkling wines! The two bowls were covered either with a wire mesh or a very attractive cane woven mesh and, if required, the metal work could be supplied silver-plated. They came in three sizes: three pints, five pints and eight pints.

Water Filters

Water filters were in general use in pubs up to about 1900, because drinking water was suspect and filtered water was required to make tea and coffee, which were popular beverages in pubs in those days. Filtered water was also heated for making punch and for drinking with brandy.

The T. Heath catalogue of 1899 lists at least a dozen different models for filtering water for restaurants, some with a capacity of fifty gallons per hour, from the main supply. The very beautiful

- CLINCHER -
SELTZOGENE

Which has quite a new method of adjusting the Tap to the Globe.

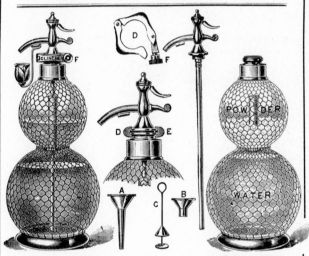

Screwing Top on and off as hitherto is entirely dispensed with.

NO MORE JAMMING OR FIXING OF
SCREWS THROUGH CORROSION.

LEAKAGES REDUCED TO A MINIMUM.

SIMPLE, RAPID, AND EFFECTIVE IN ACTION.

PRICES :

WITH ORDINARY METAL HEADS	3	5	8 pint
Wire Covered	**11/6** ...	**15/6** ...	**22/6**
Cane ,, ...	**12/6** ...	**17/-** ...	**25/6**
WITH PORCELAIN-LINED HEADS	3	5	8 pint
Wire Covered	**12/6** ...	**16/6** ...	**23/6**
Cane ,, ...	**13/6** ...	**18/-** ...	**26/6**

Silver-plated Top, 4/6 extra.   *Silver-plated Wire, 4/6 extra.*

The 'Clincher' Seltzogene from an early (c.1920) catalogue of The British Syphon Manufacturing Company Ltd.

Directions for using Seltzogenes

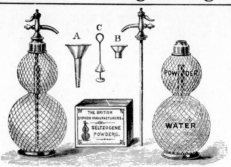

Every Beverage intended to be carbonated must be as cool as possible; the cooler it is kept the more gas is generated.

DIRECTIONS FOR USE.

1st.   Nearly fill the lower globe with water, by means of a large funnel (A), taking care that no water overflows into the upper globe.

2nd.   Remove the large funnel, replacing it by the smaller one (B), and close the tube in the upper globe with the stopper rod (C) ; pass into the upper globe a charge of tartaric acid in small crystals (white paper), and a charge of bicarbonate of soda in powder (blue paper), then remove the stopper and funnel.   It is as well to mix the two powders before putting them in the machine.

(Thus we have the water in the lower and the powders in the upper globe.)

3rd.   Insert the long tube carefully into the bottle, and screw the tap down quite tight.

4th.   Incline the apparatus a little on one side, to allow water to flow into the upper globe, till it is rather more than a third full.   Shake the machine well in a circular movement, keeping it always upright.   Two hours are sufficient for the preparation, but longer is always advantageous.   The contents are drawn by pressing down the lever.

5th.   It is advisable to draw off a wineglassful of the aerated water within a few minutes of charging, in order to release the fixed air.

IMPORTANT REMARKS.

The use of the small funnel is to prevent the powders from clogging the screw, and that of the stopper rod to prevent any powder from entering by the large tube into the lower globe while charging.

The upper globe should be as dry as possible before the machine is put in charge, and likewise the metal screw at neck, which should be well wiped.

In shaking the apparatus, care should be taken that no liquid from the upper globe passes into the lower globe.

In inserting the long glass tube, be very particular that the end is not struck against the neck or inner tube, as small bits of glass may chip off, fall into the lower globe, and get forced up into the valve, and thus cause the tap to drip. Sand or other impurity in the water will cause the same   The screw of the tap may occasionally be rubbed with a little beeswax, if found to work hard.

Be careful to let off by the tap all the carbonic acid gas before recharging the apparatus, which should be rinsed out with cold water every time ; it must not on any occasion be washed in hot water, as it would cause the glass to burst.

The powders should be kept in a dry place.

Keep the Seltzogene in a cool place, and when in charge do not place it near the fire or in the sun.

NOTICE.—The Tap of the Machine must be properly screwed down. If it is not SCREWED QUITE TIGHT the gas will escape and prevent it from working. In the "Clincher" the Clamp must be securely fixed.

Directions for using seltzogenes. From an early (c.1920) catalogue of The British Syphon Manufacturing Company Ltd.

stoneware models made by Doulton and the Berkefeld Filter Co. had capacities of up to six gallons. The catalogue also includes a report from the research laboratories of the British Medical Association implying that the Berkefeld filter would not allow the passage of organisms such as cholera and typhoid, which were evidently a danger at that time.

Water Fountains

The drinking of absinthe was banned in France after 1919 as this very strong spirit, marinated in wormwood, was the cause of severe alcoholism, blindness and impotence. A weaker range of substitutes appeared, generally called pastis, such as Pernod, Ricard and Berger.

The method of dispensing absinthe was to pour the liquid into a tumbler, over which was placed a perforated spoon on which rested a lump of sugar. This was placed beneath a water fountain

A pre-World War I water fountain at The French House in Soho. Designed to drip iced water into absinthe, which was banned in 1919, these fountains are now extremely rare.

81

containing iced water which was slowly dripped through one of four taps. An original model can be seen in use at The French House (formally The York Minster) in Dean Street, Soho, London, where Gaston Birlemont presides. M. Birlemont represents the second generation of the family who have had the pub since before World War I. Any London taxi-driver knows The French House, which was the rendezvous of all ex-patriate Frenchmen in two World Wars.

This modern water fountain is used to dispense ice-cold water for whisky. Coolness is achieved by filling the aluminium sleeve with ice cubes. In the original version, the ice floated on the water.

4 In the Bar

Advertising Models

Most pubs have advertising models decorating their back bars. These are produced mainly by distillers, cider manufacturers, brewers and others to draw attention either to their trademark or to a well-known figure which the public associates with their product.

Over the years, models have been produced in pottery, plastic and various metals. One of the earliest was the famous figure of Johnny Walker, 'Born 1820—and still going strong', and this was first produced in pottery before World War 1. It is still issued in various sizes but, from the collectors' point of view, the early models are more valuable. The author was concerned in producing a number of these in the 1950s, notably for Squire's Gin, Morland's brewery, Carlsberg and Guinness.

Morland of Abingdon have, as their brewery sign, a figure of the artist Morland, with arm outstretched and brush and palette in hand. Only 2,000 of these were produced and they are now very rare. So are the Squire's Gin models of the squire with his up-and-over twelve-bore shotgun and hi dog by his side. Only 5,000 of these were produced and not that many of them remain intact. The more popular ones, such as the many versions of the famous Babycham figure, are comparatively easy to acquire.

Also under this heading may be included some of the commemorative jugs produced by the breweries; these are generally of a distinctive shape or bear the brewery's insignia. There was a very fine series produced by Bass, the famous Burton brewery, which was more in the nature of a Toby jug (being in the shape of a civic dignitary), with the slogan 'Behind every great man there's a Worthington'. The figure has his hand behind his back, clutching a bottle of that famous brew.

The Guinness animals, such as the toucan and the penguin, were produced in both pottery and slush-moulded vinyl, the latter being a very durable material, and these can still be found, although they were produced more than twenty years ago.

*A selection of advertising models made for the brewing and distilling trades: the famous Guinness toucans (*above left*); Double Diamond (*extreme left*); Bell's Whisky flagon (*far left*); pottery model of the famous mermaid in Copenhagen, issued by Carlsberg (*left*); Johnny Walker Whisky, showing the development of the model (*above*).*

Johnny Walker. This original design by Tom Browne was commissioned in 1908 by the then director of the firm who requested that it should be 'in the likeness of my grandfather, who founded John Walker in 1820'. The famous slogan arose when the drawing was shown to another director, who coined the phrase 'Born 1820 – and still going strong!' That is as true today as in 1908.

This collection of cardboard cut-out displays shows the development of the use of the chamois figure by the makers of Babycham.

Beer Mats

In 1961, the Author co-operated with E.S. Turner of *Punch* in the production of an article called 'Dripsomania', in which he writes:

'North of the Fifty-Second Parallel, where more gracious living sets in, men and women expect a mat under their beer mug as they would expect a saucer under their tea cup.'

This very humorous article goes on to define the different types of beer mats in various countries. Even twenty years ago, there was a collector boasting that he had 26,000 different mats in his collection.

International beer-mat swapping sessions take place on the Continent and, in Britain, there is a thriving society, the British Beer Mat Collectors' Society. They have coined the word 'tegestologist' for a collector; *teges* being the Latin word for a mat or covering.

The biggest users of beer mats are the Belgians and the Germans where it is the habit to serve beer with a 'head' and to somewhat overfill the glass. Because the beer is so cold, a great deal of condensation forms on the side of the glass and runs down. It is still the custom in some bars to issue a new mat with each drink and to stack up the mats used as a tally of the number of rounds served. In other cases, the waiter will mark off the number of drinks with little ticks around the side of the beer mat. In France, the beer mats, or drip mats, are known as *sous-verres* or *sous-bock* and, in Germany, by that long descriptive word *Bierglasuntersitzer*.

Some twenty years ago, in an effort to popularise the use of beer mats south of the Trent, the author's company, which was then called Tresise's Drip Mat Co., of Burton upon Trent, organised the first beer-mat hunt. This started from The Cock Tavern in Fleet Street and finished up at a pub, now demolished, in Knightsbridge. Twelve Rank starlets started out, each accompanied by a Fleet Street columnist or well-known journalist. They were provided with a chauffeur-driven car and had to collect as many beer mats as possible along the route in two hours. They were each given half-a-dozen mats, which qualified them for a free drink in a number of selected bars en route.

One pretty young starlet, Jill Ireland, accompanied by the William Hickey of the day, went straight from Fleet Street to the Ritz Bar in Piccadilly, where they spent all their tokens on champagne cocktails, collected one beer mat and arrived dead on time, thus qualifying for a booby prize, which consisted of a nice pair of bath mats! Sabrina, a famous beauty of her day, presented the prizes. The competition for the most collected beer mat of that year was won by Babycham, who still have the winning beer mat framed and hanging in their offices at Shepton Mallet.

Collectors should remember that, although beer mats are issued free to landlords by brewers and other advertisers, they are not always in such plentiful supply that enthusiastic visitors are welcome to just walk into a bar and help themselves. It is more polite to ask for permission to have a mat and, in many cases, this will lead to the landlord producing some additional designs from behind the bar.

The earliest beer mats, produced in 1920, were of much thicker board than that used today and, in fact, the waste cuttings from the manufacture of the circular mats were repulped and moulded into mats $\frac{3}{16}$ of an inch thick. These are seldom seen nowadays and, indeed, were only produced in Belgium and Germany. Other mats are made of cork or of cellulose wadding; the latter is used to make the flimsy crinkled mats which are sometimes slipped around the bottoms of cocktail glasses. The purely functional purpose of mats has been now largely overtaken by their usefulness as an advertising medium and, whereas the earlier mats were associated with drinks being offered in a particular bar, the use of mats now has been extended to other consumables and to political slogans and, indeed, for the promotion of almost every idea. After all, from an advertiser's or publicist's point of view, it is very useful to get a message over to people as they are sitting relaxed in a bar, so that the promotional message is almost subliminal.

One of the most interesting mats was printed in 1948 to commemorate the Olympic Games held in that year. This was the first time that a six-colour drip mat had been attempted and this was produced by the author's company on cannibalised machinery at Burton upon Trent. It was for Truman's Brewery and the five concentric coloured rings formed the basic design. A total of 50,000 of these was produced (which was quite a large order in those days) and they have become one of the most desirable mats.

Another rare collector's item is the invisible ink mats which were produced for a Scottish brewery. They were printed with an invisible ink message, which could only be detected if a few drops of beer were spilt onto the mat. The message then appeared, but disappeared again when the mat dried out.

The original order for these was for half a million mats and, on the vast majority, the simple message appeared: 'Hard luck, try again', On one in every thousand mats, however, the message that appeared was: "You may have won a prize'. On the reverse of the mat was a very simple competition, which the recipient of the lucky mat completed, sent in to the brewery and, at the subsequent draw, substantial prizes were assured to the fortunate holders of the selected mats. So successful was the operation that eventually some four million mats were produced and sent up to Scotland from Burton upon Trent by private-hire car in order to get them there in time to meet the demands of the campaign. These mats are highly prized.

Interested collectors could do no better than join the British Beer Mat Collectors' Society.

Fireside Impedimenta

The central attraction of the early pubs was, of course, the fireside, with the blazing hearth to welcome a traveller on a cold and windy night. The author lived for many years in a seventeenth-century house in Hampshire which had originally been a pilgrims' rest house and later a public house. The central feature of the main living room was the enormous inglenook fireplace with a chimney stack open to the sky, above and about which the rest of the building had been constructed, as was normal in those days. There is an illustration of an inn, called The Mill, at Witherington, Gloucestershire, which shows, over the fireplace, racks for the drying-out of pipes and for the storing of muzzle-loaded guns and, in front of the fire, racks for clay pipes. Above the fire itself is a spit jack to complete the cheerful scene.

At The Three Horseshoes inn at Alveley, near Bridgnorth, Shropshire, there is quite a collection of roasting jacks and spit jacks around the fireplace and these are sometimes used for cooking in the

The fireplace at The Three Horseshoes, Alveley, near Bridgnorth, with its collection of roasting jacks and other impedimenta.

winter over the great log fire. The spit jack is often known as a bottle jack because of its shape—a cylinder with an elongated neck to hold the spindle which hangs on the hook. The early spit jacks were driven by clockwork and ran for half an hour with one revolution in each direction so that the meat or game was properly cooked all round. The earliest record of this ingenious invention is once again noted in Birmingham, in 1846, when William Lane patented a jack with two spring barrels geared to drive a spit and a few years later, in 1849, John Britten patented his roasting jack.

Before the days of gas, electric and central heating, the fireside, often an inglenook, was the central feature of a pub. In earlier days, the kitchen was the main centre of attraction in a roadside inn, being the warmest room in the house. It was perfectly usual for a large iron or copper pot to be suspended over the fire to ensure a regular supply of hot water, but the fire was also important for cooking and for this purpose the roasting jack was invented. This was a mechanical device, driven by clockwork, and consisted of a cylinder containing the clockwork, under which was suspended a spoked wheel, which usually had four hooks on which to hang game, rabbits or meat. You can find these fairly readily in country inns and there are quite a number of varieties of design. Some models incorporated a weighing balance, so that the amount hooked on could be weighed and some of these jacks would take up to forty pounds of meat or game. The chief manufacturer was Salter of Birmingham, who are still leading makers of weighing equipment.

Quite elaborate roasting devices were produced in the eighteenth and nineteenth century. At The White Hart on the riverside at Sonning-on-Thames, there is a fine device on which, of an evening, there are always half a dozen ducks, spitted onto the rotating axles of the jack, which is driven by a series of chains and gearwheels. This makes a most succulent sight for the diner.

Some of these jacks used to be geared up to a heat-activated fan which was situated in the chimney stack where the hot air of the fire made it rotate; this was connected in turn, by a series of rods, to the spit below. Sometimes the spits were turned by hand or even by a dog on a treadmill, as shown in one of Rowlandson's drawings of the kitchen of a country inn.

Other spits were forged in iron and bolted to the brickwork at the side of the inglenook and hinged, so that a variety of cooking pots could be swung over the fire.

An inglenook fireplace typical of a country pub, in this instance The Victoria Inn, Llandbedr, Gwynned.

Fireplaces and inglenooks would also have clay-pipe racks above them for drying out the pipes overnight and even clay-pipe ovens in which the pipes were baked ready for the next day's smoking session.

Nor would any open fireplace have been complete without its copper or brass chestnut roaster hanging on the wall and, while there are many attractive modern reproductions on the market, there is no comparison between them and the heavy metal roasters which were produced in the days before central heating became the fashion.

Andirons were an early and very simple form of cast-iron device used in open fireplaces to retain the logs or faggots which were the fuel in Tudor times. As architectural style changed and fireplaces were moved from the centre of the room to a place by the wall, with a chimney stack, these andirons achieved a more attractive appearance and were made in a variety of shapes and eventually included fire backs, which had charming decorations. The upright sections of the andirons were often cast in the shape of heraldic animals or human beings and, on the fire backs, there were heraldic shields or monograms of the local squire or titled-family crest.

Pokers, tongs and bellows were all very much part of fireside furniture, together with wicker or ironwork log baskets. This was in the days before coal superseded wood as a more suitable burning material. The designs of bellows were quite ingenious; some were operated by hand and others by foot pedals and these make a very interesting subject for a collection.

Furniture

The eighteenth century was famous for its taverns and its coffee houses. London inns at which the coaches and post-chaises were wont to call were also places where traders and their customers met to transact business. It was at this time that the furnishings of public-house rooms graduated from the rough and ready benches and high-backed settles to the more elaborate joinery furniture which became a feature of both the town and country inn. The leading stylists in the creation of the new furniture where Sheraton, Chippendale and Hepplewhite, but the coming of the Industrial Revolution produced a lower grade of craftsman who relied on mechanised production to produce vast quantities of indifferent furniture for the blossoming public houses and clubs of the time. Nevertheless, the type of furnishing then in vogue has become a desirable collectors' item and the four-poster bed and brass bedsteads, huge wardrobes and marble-topped washstands now appear in many a modern flat.

Glass—Ornate, Etched and Engraved

The use of highly-decorated glass for pub design was very much in vogue in early Victorian days in the famous era of the gin palaces. These beautifully-executed glass panels were used as mirrors, fanlights, windows and snob screens. Prior to 1851, there was a punishing tax on window glass, but after the repeal of this duty, the use of glass panels became within the reach of most licensees and pub designers.

It was in 1851 that Sir Joseph Paxton built the then considered to be miraculous Crystal Palace, which was an absolute wonder of curved and decorated glass panels. The patterns were etched into the surface of the plate glass by rubbing it over with fine emery cloth and the panels which were produced were comparatively small. It was in 1850 that a Bristol firm, Mark Bowden, adopted an American system, which enabled them to hold large sheets of glass upright and then use a rotating stone grinding-wheel to create designs. This led to improved techniques which brought the price of engraved glass within the reach of most designers. Further technical developments in acid etching, whereby fluoric acid was poured into the pattern, which was traced out of 'Brunswick Black', enabled much more intricate designs to be produced. By 1860, these often took the form of very complex drawings of birds, peacocks, swans and storks and lovely curvaceous shapes which appealed to the etcher's art. By 1870, the technique arrived of back-painting in colour on the etched or embossed glass and some beautiful mirrors of the late nineteenth century and early twentieth century can still be found in the old pubs.

Around 1880, a patent was taken out for sand blasting designs into the plate glass, using zinc stencils to create the actual patterns. A whole variety of intensities of frostings were available, which again improved the possibilities from the artist's point of view.

The major breweries and distilleries produced some really beautiful designs, strongly influenced by the Art Nouveau movement and many of these survive to this day; some of them are very large, up to twelve feet high or long.

Labels

It has been said that the first label was a fig leaf! It certainly served the purpose of drawing attention to the object which was on offer, which is the prime object of labelling.

Collectors of beer, soft drink and wine labels can do no better than become members of the Labologist's Society, whose current address is given at the end of the book. The Society is entirely concerned with the collection of beer-bottle labels from this country and abroad and their excellent guide gives a mass of useful information to anyone interested in this subject. They also organise exchange and sale between collectors who are members and they issue a newsletter from time to time.

The earliest labels used in the drink industry were probably those on port wine in the middle of the eighteenth century, but it was not until a hundred years later that the modern type of bottle appeared and it was a legal requirement for these to bear a paper label.

Beer-bottle labels also came into use in about the middle of the nineteenth century, prior to which time beer was supplied mainly in bulk in the barrel. At the beginning of this century, there were hundreds of small breweries up and down the country, each producing a variety of labels for their products and these early examples are extremely rare.

In the early 1900s, the law required that bottles of beer, sold for the take-home trade, had to have a strap label over the cork or stopper to prevent children having a quick swig on the way home with daddy's pint!

The best known of all beer labels is, of course, the famous Bass red triangle for their pale ale. An executive of the brewery sat all night on the steps of the registrar's office when the first trade marks were being allocated and thus the Bass red triangle is, in fact, Trade Mark No. 1; their diamond trade mark was the second entry and became Trade Mark No. 2. The same famous trade mark achieved further fame when a bottle of Bass, showing the red triangle, was included in a painting, dated 1821, entitled 'Bar at the Folies Bergère', by Edouard Manet.

The design of beer-bottle labels has become highly sophisticated in recent years. The author is still British representative of a company (Illochroma S.A.) in Belgium, which is the largest producer of beer-bottle labels on the Continent. This company goes to great lengths to produce labels which have hard-hitting power on the back-bar, or on the shelf of the supermarket, and employs teams of psychologists who study public reaction to different designs. In its design studios, there is very advanced equipment to measure the reaction of the eye to the colour and design and to the readability of labels when seen under varying conditions at the point-of-sale. Continental labels differ generally from the British-produced label, in that they are printed on what we call 'wet strength' paper, which is very difficult to tear. The quality of this paper makes for a better printing surface and superior properties of adhesion and positioning on the bottle, but the de-labelling requires a different type of washing machine in the bottling stores and, at the moment, this is not a practical proposition in Britain. In this country, the brewers have a bottle-exchange agreement and, therefore, a number of foreign bottles may end up in a brewery bottling line, all with different labels. These have to be washed off and the bottle cleaned and sterilised before the bottle goes for refilling. If a proportion of wet strength labels which would not come off the bottle were to be introduced, this would cause immense trouble in the bottling department. Collectors who acquire continental labels can fairly easily spot the difference in paper quality.

The true collector will prefer to acquire the label by purchasing a bottle of the actual beer and then steaming off the label. The method recommended by the Labologist's Society is simply to submerge the bottle in a bowl of very hot water, to which a little bit of salt has been added, until the label comes off and then to place the label between two pieces of cardboard held together with elastic bands so that it will dry flat.

If collectors are trying to acquire a collection quite quickly, then they can write to the various breweries, but a stamped addressed envelope should always be enclosed because the breweries do get a very large number of requests for samples, particularly when new labels are issued. The handbook issued by the Labologist's Society gives an extensive list of the various shapes of bottle labels, which will assist the collector to categorise his stock. This may in itself be a difficult job when one realises that the Secretary of the Society has 21,000 different British beer labels and this is listed in the *Guinness Book of Records* as the largest collection of its kind in the world.

Lustreware

Lustreware is a kind of pottery which has a rather leatherlike appearance and is mainly found in Sussex where this attractive material was made from the local clay in the Walden Valley, where it has been in manufacture for hundreds of years.

Originally, the local potteries produced chimney pots, tiles and dairy vessels, but in the nineteenth century, as the coastal resorts began to achieve fame as fashionable watering places, the potteries started to make souvenirs. It was during the 1920s and 1930s that Dicker pottery became a highly collectable item from this part of the country. Then they made not only drinking vessels and jugs but also candlesticks and ashtrays, and flower bowls in the form of the local 'trug' baskets. The potters also made reproductions of early Roman and English shapes in what they called 'Sussex Iron'. Pottery manufactured before the turn of this century was rarely given any date mark, but from 1900 onwards the bases were marked with either 'UC' or 'N' or the words 'Dicker Sussex' on the base.

Since World War 2, the pottery has been closed and there is now no trace of it, but local collectors are now keenly acquiring specimens of the old Sussex pottery and no doubt this very unusual and attractive ware will become a valuable collectors' item.

Musical Instruments

Pubs have had so-called 'piped-music' for considerably longer than the modern tape- or disc-recorded entertainment. The earliest forms of what were called 'automata' appeared from about the 1600s onwards and were mainly in private ownership. Where these ingenious gadgets played musical instruments, they were termed 'androids', which sounds rather like a word from the new space-age technology. A certain J. Vaucanson, who lived in the eighteenth century, made quite remarkable mechanical music players and even constructed a life-size duck, which not only made all the noises that a duck can make, but went through the motions of a living duck, including preening, shaking its wings, dabbling in the water, eating, digestion and excretion, but not, alas, reproduction. He made only one of these and it was on show in London for many years.

Another instrument maker of about the same time was Pierre Jacquet-Dorz, who produced a tall and beautiful maiden sitting at a small organ, on which she played an old French melody. This she achieved in the orthodox way by depressing the keys with her fingers as her hands moved over the keyboard, her bosom heaving with emotion and, at the end of the performance, she rose and bowed to the audience. These instruments date from 1770. It was at a later stage that the first musical boxes and automatic pianos appeared and these are still to be seen in quite a number of pubs. Generally these worked either from a cylinder, or barrel, on which prongs plucked at the tuned pins, or from metal discs, where the prongs projected to play the tune.

The cone of musical teeth was first produced by Antoine Saver in Switzerland in about 1790 and it is not surprising that it was the Swiss watch- and clock-makers who invented this type of movement. Around 1890, the first musical instruments playing from reels of card or paper and using compressed air appeared and these became very popular in public houses. Symphoniums, as these were called, became immensely popular and can still be seen, particularly in Belgium and Holland, as can the polyphons.

Polyphons, which now command quite a high price, were only produced for comparatively few years and there is a shop in the Portobello Road, in London, which specialises in the restoration and sale of these fascinating instruments. For people interested in collecting these, the best handy reference book is *Discovering Mechanical Music*, issued by Shire Publications Ltd.

There are quite a number of books on the subject of barrel organs, mechanical music players and so on, and many museums show examples. There are also a number of societies concerned with the subject, including the Music Box Society of Great Britain, which can be contacted at 40 Station Approach, Hayes, Bromley, Kent.

Pub Games

The oldest of all the tavern games is undoubtedly chess. The design of chess boards and the methods of playing have changed very little over the centuries and the chequers is certainly one of the very oldest and most frequently found sign boards. In the ruins of ancient Pompeii, the sign of a chequer board was found outside a tavern and this was probably the very first subject ever depicted on an inn sign. In earlier days, chess boards were made in precious metals for the rich but the ordinary man's chess board would have been of wood; elm is often mentioned in the old records.

Somewhat simpler than chess, draughts was a popular tavern game and also a game called 'tables', which is the old name for what we now call backgammon which, in recent years, has achieved great popularity. Early illustrations of backgammon boards show that they have remained virtually unchanged over the centuries.

Another early pub game was shovelboard, which was a large-scale version of what is now known as shove ha'penny. A lot of these games were engraved onto slates or onto the bar top or a table top. Shovelboard, however, required virtually a separate room and Joseph Strutt, in his book *Sports and Pastimes of the People of England*, talks about:

'a low public house in Benjamin Street, near Clerkenwell Green, where the Shovelboard is almost 3 ft in breadth and 39 ft 2 in in length'.

This is, of course, about the same length as a modern skittle alley which, once more, is based on a much earlier game. But shove ha'penny, or shovegroat as it was known in the sixteenth century, is now generally played on a portable board, which can be placed on a table or bar top.

A rare pub game is called Swanage board and is a longer version of shove ha'penny, played exclusively in the Swanage area of Dorset. On Thursday nights, a dozen or more pubs in the Isle of Purbeck play out their league matches. The board is 5 ft 6 in long and the game is played only with Guernsey or Irish half-pennies. The very highly-polished mahogany or teak table is buffed-up with soda-water and acquires, over the years, a surface so smooth that the coins slide the four or more feet with only the slightest shove. The scoring area of the board (see illustration) allows 101-up or a variety of other games to be played. It is almost impossible to acquire one of these boards, which are carefully guarded, and woe betide the player who rests a hand or even a finger on the board on match night!

Another popular pub game which can still be found today in certain parts of the country is Nine Men's Morris, which is a board game. The most popular kind of pub game at present is darts and

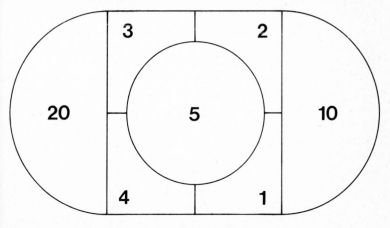

Diagram of the scoring area on a Swanage board.

the whole business is now very highly organised into leagues and competitions and has become quite a big commercial enterprise.

The memorabilia which collectors can acquire in connection with all these pub games is really limited to shove ha'penny and other board games.

Smokiana

King James I, writing in 1603, said of tobacco:

'A custom loathsome to the eye, harmful
to the brain, dangerous to the lungs and in
the black stinking fumes thereof, nearest
resembling the horrible Stygian smoke of
the pit which is bottomless.'

Nevertheless, ten years later, there were 6,000 shops in and around London selling tobacco and the taxes they paid no doubt went a long way to soothing the Monarch's anger at the lack of response to his 'Counterblasts to Tobacco'. His sincerity may be gauged by the granting, for cash paid into his own purse, of a monopoly to the Worshipful Company of Clay Pipe Manufacturers. In 1850, there were twenty factories in Lincolnshire alone making clay pipes, yet, by 1900, there was only one survivor, at Grantham, and, by 1950, there was only one factory in the Potteries supplying pipes for a cool smoke.

The word 'Smokiana' was first used in 1890 by R.T. Pritchett, who wrote a book called *Ye Smokiana*, so it will be seen that this word is already nearly one hundred years old in usage and was, perhaps, the forerunner of many other generic terms for collectables, such as 'Breweriana', 'Militaria', 'Victoriana'.

Readers who are interested in collecting the paraphernalia associated with 'the weed' could do no better than to start with a visit to the unique and fascinating House of Pipes Museum at Bramber, near Steyning in Sussex. You can see there a collection of 25,000 items from one hundred and fifty countries, covering no less than 1,500 years of history.

Smoking and snuff taking have always been associated with taverns and pubs and, indeed, are very much social habits, rather akin to drinking. Few people go into a pub simply to have a drink and, likewise, in days gone by, smoking clubs and smoke rooms were very much a part of the pub scene.

Tobacco Jars and Cutters

When tobacco was first imported into this country, it came in leaf form and was not already cured and packed. Containers were required and these took the form of tobacco jars at the point-of-sale and were made in pewter, china, brass, iron and lead. They were a very popular presentation item from the mid-eighteenth century onwards. They had to be tightly sealed, often with a lead liner, in order to keep in the essential flavour and aroma of the tobacco and often had a handle moulded in the form of a negro's head to associate the product with the country of origin of the weed. Early examples of these containers are comparatively rare but they make an interesting collection. At a later date, tobacco was packed in decorative tins and, at the House of Pipes Museum, there can be seen an enormous collection of decorative tobacco tins dating from the nineteenth century.

Collectors may also come across the tobacco cutters, which were used for chopping off lengths of plug, though these were generally used in tobacconist shops rather than in public houses.

Pipes and Tampers

Having bought the tobacco, a pipe was required in order to smoke it. The history of pipes is in itself quite a fascinating subject and pipes are a popular collectors' item.

From the nineteenth century, the clay pipe was predominant and, indeed, in the period 1860–1870, there were no less than nine hundred clay-pipe manufacturers in this country. Some of the pipes were extremely decorative and they varied in length from a quite short 3- or 4-inch pipe, up to the long 24-inch churchwarden, so beloved of Dickens and his contemporaries.

Ancestors of the author were in the clay-pipe manufacturing business in Market Rasen, in Lincolnshire, in the middle of the nineteenth century and some interesting family records show the price which the outworkers were paid for making the pipes for the wholesalers and retailers. Payment for making the pipes was by piecework. For pipes 18 to 24 inches long, an outworker was paid one shilling a gross, for the 10-inch ones or 'dandies', he received ninepence a gross and, for the short 'cutties', sevenpence halfpenny a gross. He had to make sixteen dozen to the gross in order to allow for breakages.

Pipes were sold for prices varying from one farthing to two pence each and public houses supplied them free to customers. A jarful would be kept on the counter and the squeamish smoker would break off the last inch so he could get a clean start to his smoke. It was also customary to leave them in wrought-iron or cast-iron cradles left hanging over the fire at night so that they would be sterilised for the next day's patrons.

The collecting of clay pipes and fragments has become more popular in recent years. Following the introduction of metal detectors, many enthusiasts are digging away on old bottle-tips and in yards behind old pubs and here thousands of fragments of clay pipes are unearthed and, occasionally, a good sample comes up complete.

It was customary for fishermen going out with the trawlers to take two or three dozen clay pipes with them on a trip to sea, which is not surprising when one realises how brittle and expendable a clay pipe was.

The metal moulds which were used for the shaping of these clay pipes included an embossed pattern with the maker's name or initials on the bowl. At the factory in Market Rasen, one of a hundred pipe makers in Lincolnshire alone, they had forty different patterns, including ships, flags, acorns and patriotic figures. Sometimes, the bowl itself would be shaped like a man's face, with the tobacco filling his open top hat. A pipe-maker in Lancashire has 400 old moulds still in use.

It was customary to have pipe-smoking contests at village fetes and the veterans would be given a churchwarden and a whole pound of tobacco and there was a prize for the smoker who had the longest staying power. Tobacco in those days was three pence an ounce, yet in 1589 it was three shillings an ounce! In 1614, the Court of the Star Chamber imposed a duty of six shillings and ten pence per pound on tobacco. Cultivation of tobacco was prohibited by an Act of Charles II in 1684.

Enthusiasts who like to collect pipes should always, when they have the opportunity, look in the eaves and the roofs of old houses, because workmen often put down their pipes and forgot them while the building of the house was in progress.

The clay pipe began to go out of fashion towards the end of the nineteenth century as briars and other types of pipe came in. The collection of meerschaum and other decorative pipes is a subject in itself and in the Bibliography there are references listed for those

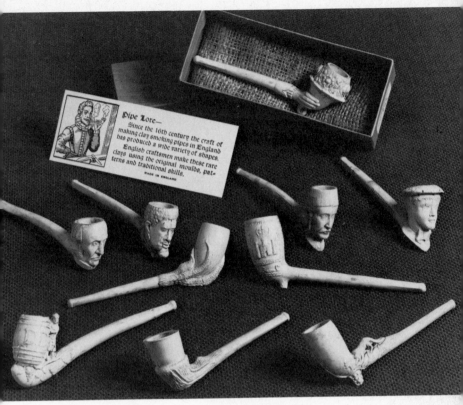

Clay pipes made from old moulds still being used in Manchester.

who wish to go deeper into this form of collecting.

Having put the tobacco into the pipe, it then needed to be tamped and there is a very wide range of different forms of tamper which can be picked up quite cheaply in bric-a-brac shops and elsewhere. These look rather like a seal and, indeed, they were sometimes used both as a tamper to press down the tobacco and a seal for stamping on the wax which sealed correspondence. Some of these tampers are extremely attractive and quite expensive to buy when made of silver, but they are also available in brass, ivory and, very often, in the shape of well-known symbolic figures, such as the Lincoln Imp.

Because pipe-smoking was a male-oriented hobby, many designs were of an erotic nature, such as the phallic emblem of Priapus or a lady's leg, with a stocking moulded or cut into the carving at the top. Items of this sort, which are quite small and easy to display, make a fascinating collection.

Towards the end of the nineteenth century came the introduction of the paper-wrapped cigarette and the decline of snuff taking and, to some extent, of pipe smoking, but certainly of smoking from clay pipes.

Snuff and Snuff Taking

One of the most important derivatives of the tobacco leaf is snuff and this has a most interesting history. Snuff taking was frowned upon by Queen Victoria but thrived mightily, particularly in the earlier part of this century. Not since 1590 has there been a tobacco product that did not carry excise duty but, in January 1978, in order to comply with EEC regulations, the excise duty was removed completely on tobacco intended entirely for the manufacture of snuff and this has led to a dramatic increase in the demand for snuff in Great Britain.

When Columbus made his second voyage of discovery at the end of the fifteenth century, he was accompanied by Ramon Pane, who took note of the habits of Indians in the New World. Among the novelties he observed was the use of tobacco, either by smoking or sniffing. It rapidly spread throughout Europe and, to start with, the habit of sniffing snuff spread more rapidly than that of smoking. In England, however, smoking came first, to be succeeded by snuff taking. The introduction of tobacco to England has been variously attributed to Hawkins, Lane, Drake and Raleigh, but in popular legend, the credit is given to Raleigh and, at that time, it was advocated as a measure against contagion and medicinally recommended for headaches, insomnia, toothache, coughs and colds.

The Golden Age of Snuff Taking was during the Regency period when the future King George IV, then the Prince Regent, and his one-time favourite, Beau Brummel, were leading exponents of the habit. All the favourite characters of the eighteenth century were inveterate snuffers. Dr Johnson, as one would expect, had some pertinent things to say. He did not carry his snuff in a box, but in a special pocket made of leather, which he had stitched into his waistcoats. Tradesmen of that time tended to have a snuff box made with reference to their trade, so that a shoemaker would carry a box in the form of a shoe; an innkeeper, a barrel; a coachman, a horse's hoof; and even the undertaker had a miniature coffin complete with sliding lid, made into a snuff box!

Another type of snuff box was one carried in a gold-topped walking-stick. The young man-about-town often felt incompletely attired unless he had his snuff box with him and it was considered very smart to have one embodied in his cane.

The ladies of the period were equally adept at the art of snuff taking and, at Bath, it was customary to have snuff boxes floating in a dish, together with a handkerchief for use, whilst the bathers were disporting themselves in the medicinal waters. The high prices paid for these snuff boxes can be imagined when one learns that, when George IV was crowned, he paid £8,000 for snuff boxes to present to foreign visitors.

George IV was a great collector of snuff boxes and collected several hundreds of these in gold and jewelled finishes. Queen Victoria converted many of them into personal jewellery because she so strongly objected to snuff taking. We read that Lord Petersham bought nearly one hundredweight of snuff at the auction of the stock of snuff at Windsor Castle when George IV died. He had a snuff box for every day of the year and would make his daily choice to match the weather and the company he was keeping and then not use it again for at least a year. When he died, the value of the snuff he left was £3,000.

The most fascinating shop remaining in London today is probably Friborg and Treyer, who have left their original bow-fronted shop in the Haymarket and moved to the House of Bewlay at 214 Piccadilly, where a variety of brands of snuff are on sale.

Some of the eighteenth-century snuff boxes are fetching very high prices indeed. A Battersea enamel box bought for £2 in the 1920s fetched 600 guineas in the 1960s; one made in 1744 fetched 16,000 guineas and one in gold, tortoiseshell and diamonds made £23,000. Yet quite attractive snuff boxes can still be found at reasonable prices in the antique markets.

It was customary to present an engraved and decorated snuff box in gold or silver to personages of importance to commemorate significant events.

One can pick up snuff-spoons and measures. These are small spoons with tiny bowls which, if very small, were used to scoop up a portion of snuff to be sniffed up the nostrils or, in the case of those with slightly larger bowls, about one-half the capacity of a teaspoon, as a measure by which snuff was sold. In a Gentleman's Club, it was, and still is, customary to have a snuff horn on the table in the entrance hall. This was generally a pair of ram's horns with a silver or pewter snuff box set between them. Such items now command quite a high price. Another item for collectors are snuff rasps. These generally date back to the late seventeenth or early eighteenth century and were made in embossed silver, ivory and exotic woods and their convex covers were beautifully decorated. They were used for rasping the snuff from wads of dry tobacco and many snuff takers, such as Dean Swift, favoured a rasp in order to be sure of getting fresh snuff when they needed it. These rasps, however, are quite rare and one would generally expect to pay quite a high price for them.

Cigarette Cards

There are many items associated with cigarettes which are of interest to collectors, such as cigarette cards. These were first used by Wills as stiffeners for the paper packets in about 1887 and rapidly became one of the most collected items until around 1939, when, at the beginning of World War 2, they were dropped on the grounds of economy and have never really appeared in volume since then. There are many well-known collections of cigarette cards and also of cigarette and cigar cases.

Cigar Bands, Boxes and Cutters

In connection with cigars, a whole range of cigar cutters were produced and some of the earlier ones were most ornate and decorative. Also, various types of cigar boxes were available, fitted with humidors to keep the leaves in good condition. Cigar bands, the papers around the cigar at the point where the fingers normally hold the cigar, make a very nice framed display for collectors. The original idea of the cigar band was to protect the cigar from soiled or sweaty fingers and also to carry an advertising message denoting the grade and quality of the cigar itself.

Lighting Tobacco

At the time when matches were comparatively expensive and people used vestas and various types of tinder-box to light their pipes, it was common enough to see spill holders hanging alongside a candle by the fire. Some of these were quite ornate and made in brass, copper or pottery. Long wrought-iron tongs were used to pluck a red-hot coal from the fire to light a clay pipe.

The methods of lighting tobacco, whether a pipe, cigar or cigarette, were many and collections of early fuses, vestas and tinder boxes are most interesting, as are early samples of the wooden match boxes and carton match boxes.

Prior to the introduction of the petrol lighter, round about 1930, almost every pub would have a match-striker on the bar. These were made in a variety of materials and some of them were most attractive and are now a collectors' item. They held vestas or what are known as 'strike anywhere' matches, as opposed to the later safety matches which would only strike on a special surface. These match holders were made in silver, brass, iron and tin, papier mâché, glass, china and wood. Examples of those which advertised whisky, soft drinks and other products have become much sought after.

The bookmatch, which was introduced in about 1935, has also become a simple and inexpensive item for collection and these are very colourful. They are now made in many countries and in a very wide variety of printings and the quality of some of the printing on the fairly modern samples is really quite superb. They are produced to commemorate special events or as advertising for tourist centres or individual pubs and restaurants.

Advertising Material

Advertising ephemera has become a much collected item and some of the show cards and advertising plaques produced by the tobacco companies are very attractive, ranging from those produced on tinplate and enamelled surfaces to cardboard. Along with wall decorations are advertising ashtrays and advertising models generally.

Collectors of ephemera connected with cigarette smoking should try to get hold of a copy of the centenary book produced by John Player & Sons of Nottingham in 1977. In it, are beautifully printed examples of early cigarette cards and advertising material in full colour.

Spittoons

Last but not least of the paraphernalia connected with the sale of tobacco in its various forms are spittoons, also known as cuspidors.

At one stage of our social history every household had spittoons and these were produced in brass or copper and sometimes in lead, but quite frequently in china or other ceramic materials. They generally did not carry any advertising message for obvious reasons, but are now collected and used for flower displays or even as ashtrays. Since the introduction of laws which were designed to discourage spitting, these interesting items are no longer to be found in public houses.

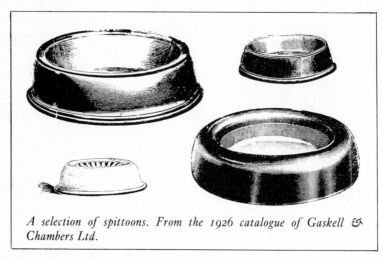

A selection of spittoons. From the 1926 catalogue of Gaskell & Chambers Ltd.

Yards and Boots of Ale

In the days of Queen Elizabeth I, it was possible to go into any large inn and order a yard of ale, and this was often referred to as an 'ell' glass, the ell being the measure of approximately one yard and nine inches.

Yards of ale have no feet to support them and were certainly in use at the coronation of James II. The diarist, John Evelyn, tells that the High Sheriff of Kent would drink his loyal toast from nothing else.

By the eighteenth century, the yard had somewhat changed in style and taken on the shape which is currently in use. The right way to drink from a yard is to tilt the vessel very slowly until the liquid has emptied the bowl to the point where the locked-out air can enter; otherwise there is a surge which catches the unwary drinker in full-flow!

5 Miscellaneous Collectables

Advertising Material and Brewers' Booklets

Most breweries have, from time to time, issued booklets, in some cases quite expensive productions, tracing the history of their breweries and these make a fascinating collection for breweriana enthusiasts. Also, the major breweries usually issue a house magazine on a monthly or quarterly basis and these too are well worth collecting, as also are the annual balance sheets and statements of account issued by the large national brewers such as Bass, who, in their annual statement, give quite a lot of space to an analysis of the Group's activities, and of their attitudes and responsibilities to the public and the ramifications of their organisation.

A very interesting booklet, entitled *Three Centuries*, was produced by Barclay, Perkins & Co. Ltd at their Southwark Brewery in south-east London. This tells a fascinating story and copies of it are still available. Bass, in Burton upon Trent, run their famous museum of brewing which is by far the best of its kind which the Author, who has visited brewing museums throughout Europe, has ever seen. The souvenir shop and book shop and the whole trip around the brewery is very worthwhile.

Some of the smaller breweries also produce interesting literature including Theakston's brewery at Masham in Yorkshire and Wadworth's at Devizes in Wiltshire, who have both produced beautifully illustrated explanatory publications. The Brewers' Society produces a quarterly review which is well illustrated and most informative.

For those interested in the history of cider making, there is a book written by the former curator of the Museum of Cider in Hereford, M. Quignon, and the history of cider making in Devonshire is very charmingly described in a book issued by Henley's, which is based at Abbotskerswell but has depots throughout the West Country. Hall and Woodhouse of Blandford in Dorset also have a very useful little quick guide to Badger Beer.

There is very little advertising material or ephemera available to

These two solid brass wall plaques were first manufactured in Birmingham in the late 1950s. The stamping dies weigh 14 cwt each!

Advertising plaque in polychrome stoneware designed by Kruger-Gray for Greene King Breweries and produced by Royal Doulton Potteries.

the collector from prior to about 1840. It was at about that time that the development of the railway system enabled the provincial brewers, such as Bass and Allsop in Burton upon Trent, to expand their market beyond the immediate region in which they could deliver by horse-drawn transport. Prior to that, the Burton breweries had shipped beer down the River Trent, which was then navigable, to Hull, whence it was taken to Europe and as far afield as the USSR. The ever-expanding British Empire demanded beers which would travel out to India by boat; hence the origin of the famous India Pale Ale (IPA), which was produced for this purpose.

With the advent of national distribution came the need for advertising, both through the mass media and at the point-of-sale, and one of the earliest forms of advertising was the highly-decorated, engraved and coloured glass mirrors, which adorned the gin palaces and bars of the mid-nineteenth century.

Agricultural Implements

Rural pubs have always been associated with rural crafts, hence the very large numbers of pubs called The Plough, The Blacksmith, The Farmer's Arms, etc. so the collecting of agricultural implementa is naturally associated with the country inn.

The plough has always been the most useful and important piece of equipment on the farm and was manufactured jointly by the local wheelwright and the village blacksmith. In the early nineteenth century, the use of the all-iron plough became universal and continued until the mechanisation of farming between the two great Wars. There are a large number of books on the subject and, for those interested in collecting ploughs and ploughshares, undoubtedly the best is a series on horsedrawn farm vehicles by John Thompson, all of which deal with country crafts and are invaluable for the intending collector.

A fine collection of agricultural implements can be seen at The Plough, which is to be found at Robins Bottom Cottage near Iping, Midhurst, West Sussex. The proprietor, Anne Smithells, has built up her collection in a beautifully reconstructed barn over many years and has a number of interesting items for sale.

Of course, not everyone can collect such large pieces of equipment as ploughs, harrows, turnip drills and the like and more popular subjects for collection associated with country crafts are

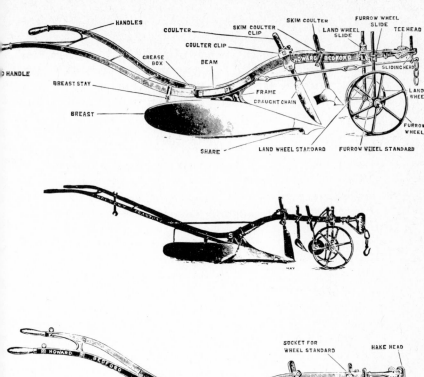

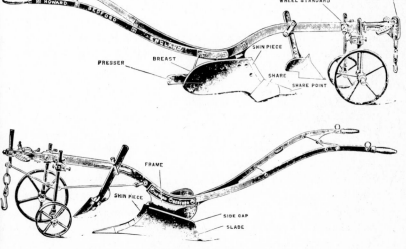

Detailed drawings of horse-drawn ploughs showing the working parts. From top to bottom: *Ordinary Wheeled Plough; English Plough; Chilled Breast Digging Ploughs.*

113

farmers' tools, pitchforks, hay rakes, etc and, most of all, horse brasses and harness decorations.

Shepherds' equipment is as fascinating as any other rural craftsman's tools. Up until 1800, the wealthiest industry in England was sheep-farming. Great fortunes were built up from the immense herds of sheep that were reared in the Cotswolds, Welsh hills and Kentish Wealds. The shepherd was a greatly respected workman and, with his distinctive crook, he would stand out at any annual Hiring Fair. Crooks came in many styles—neck crooks, leg crooks, dipping crooks—each designed for a special purpose. Then there were the sheep-shearing tools, scissors and dags, trimming saws for distorted horns, salve boxes for ointments, and horns for administering medicines to sick animals. Sheep collars with protruding bars prevented animals from escaping through broken hedges or turning their heads to lick sores. The shepherd would spend long, lonely days in the open and would carry a wooden cask of ale or cider, variously called a firkin, beaver or costrel. All these accoutrements may be found in village inns.

Terry Keegan, at the Country Centre, Clows Top, near Kidderminster, has one of the very few large collections of seats from agricultural implements. For many readers, this might call to mind the seats on a modern tractor but, in fact, these cast-iron relics of early days of agricultural machinery go back for many years and are quite ornately patterned; most of them have built into the pattern the name of the manufacturer, e.g. Bamford. Terry has about sixty of these seats decorating his large barn show room and regularly exchanges them with American seat collectors. The Cast Iron Seat Collectors Association of America has a very thick catalogue, listing literally hundreds of different designs and these are very much sought after as a form of indoor decoration for hunting and fishing lodges. They can also be converted into bar seats, although one wonders what would happen to a young lady who returned home with 'Bamford' embossed on her bottom!

A British Society of enthusiasts has now been formed and particulars can be obtained from Terry Keegan who has just published a book entitled *Take a Seat—The Cast Iron Seats of Great Britain and Ireland*.

Shire Publications have produced a selection of books, including

Agricultural implement seats from the collection of Terry Keegan.

Old Farm Tools, Discovering Horse Brasses and *The Village Blacksmith* (see Bibliography). These little books, costing about £1 each, are an excellent guide for the beginner who is looking for a subject to collect.

Beer Tokens

Napoleon called the British 'a Nation of shopkeepers' and it was the growth of the small independent business in the Victorian era which led to the proliferation of all kinds of advertising materials. One such advertisement was the circulation of little metal discs or checks, bearing the name and address of a tradesman and of his services. These were vary largely used by hotels and public houses and were known as beer tokens or tickets. The first of these beer tokens appeared around 1850 and they were in continual use right up to 1914. On one side would be the name and address of the pub or publican and on the reverse would be a large figure indicating the value of the token; this would range from one halfpenny to as high as one shilling. The actual purpose for which these tokens were distributed is not absolutely certain but it could have been for any one of several, apart from the obvious advertising value.

Gambling for cash in public houses was illegal under the 1845 Gaming Act so these tokens could have been purchased from the publican and used as an alternative to money; or they may have been used as prizes in games such as darts, skittles and dominoes. For those public houses which had entertainments or bowling greens, a small entrance fee would perhaps be charged and this refunded in the form of tokens which could be used to obtain drink or tobacco, rather like some pubs today charge for car parking but will exchange the car-parking ticket at the bar for beverages or other goods. Again, they may have been used to pay casual labour at a discount and it has even been suggested that wives bought a supply of these tokens on pay day and then rationed their husbands' drinking during the week.

Not many of these tokens remain because they were stamped and engraved on good quality metal and, as this had a high scrap value, most of them have been melted down over the years. Some of the most interesting collections can be seen in Lincolnshire, at the Usher Gallery, in Lincoln, and at the museums of Grantham, Peterborough and Spalding, or in the USA at the collection of Dr Neil B. Todd of Newtonville, Massachusetts.

Part of a collection of beer tokens from the Lincoln Museum, Lincolnshire.

Corn Dollies

There are many interesting agricultural items to be found in village inns and corn dollies are often found decorating the bar, especially at harvest time when the 'last handful' of corn is often reserved for making these favours. They are usually fashioned by local amateur crafts folk.

Horn Ware

Horn has been described as 'man's first plastic' and has been used to make a variety of items often found in pubs, e.g. drinking horns, snuff dispensers, shoe horns. Horn grows naturally on the heads of animals and the backs of tortoises, as well as forming the hooves of horses, feathers of birds and our own finger nails! It is a versatile material and articles of horn make a delightful collection. Home of the present industry is in Westmorland at the Abbey Horn Works in Kendal, who publish a useful little book about themselves.

Horse Brasses and Saddlery

Horse brasses are by far the most popular form of collection connected with agriculture. Brasses have been made over the years to commemorate almost every great event: coronations, weddings, battles and victories, famous people and religious feasts. There is almost no limit to the variety which can be found.

The current Birmingham production of horse brasses runs into hundreds of thousands a year. This is not to suggest that these are not a collectable item, although they are modern reproductions, but the best brasses are those which have actually seen service on the martingale or leatherwork of a working horse. Experience will soon show that the special patina and smoothness, achieved by many years of rubbing, cannot be successfully imitated by mechanical means. On old cast brasses, little cast marks, where the metal has been poured into the mould, protrude or have been worn smooth with years of wear. Most prized of all are the brasses with a ceramic centre. Modern reproduction brasses are stamped out and are easily identifiable as such.

However, no one should be completely content with collecting just horse brasses, although they are attractive and easy to display. There are also other harness decorations which adorn a well-turned

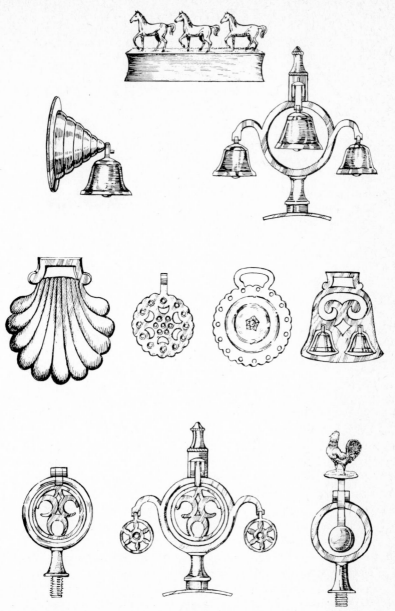

A selection of harness decorations. From top to bottom: *face piece; bell terrets; horse brasses; fly terrets.*

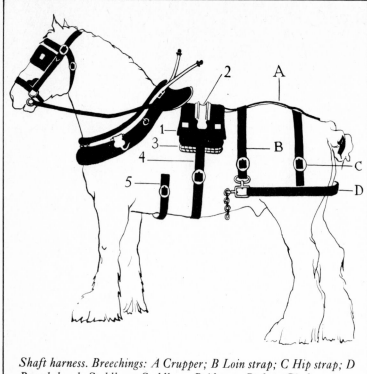

Shaft harness. Breechings: A Crupper; B Loin strap; C Hip strap; D Breech band. Saddle: 1 Saddle; 2 Bridge; 3 Pad; 4 Girth strap; 5 Belly band.

out horse, albeit a heavy shire horse used for pulling ploughs or a lighter steed for transport purposes. The accompanying illustrations show some of the more delightful collectables: rosettes, bell terrets and face pieces, hame plates and fly terrets and then the pieces of the harness—the hames, the chains and the buckles, and the bits and stirrups and snaffles.

Again, one of the best collections can be seen at the Country Centre at Clows Top (see p. 114) where the proprietor, Terry Keegan, has many interesting articles for sale, as well as being the author of a number of books on the subject of the heavy horse. These and a number of other books on the history of horse brasses are listed in the Bibliography and anyone intending to build up a collection is recommended to obtain one of them.

Horse-Shoes

Horse-shoes date back to Roman times and a country pub can hardly exist which does not have at least one hanging on an old oak beam. There is a never-ending controversy about which way up they should be nailed on the wall. If upright, with the horns in the air, they are said 'to keep the luck in' and if with the horns downwards, they are said to 'stop the luck running out'.

The earliest horse-shoes were called 'hippo-sandals' and Cleopatra is said to have had her favourite donkeys fitted with gold shoes! Collecting horse-shoes only became fashionable early this century. Presumably they were so common until the era of the motor car that no one thought of them as a collectors' item!

Horse-shoe throwing as a sport is somewhat akin to skittles. Popular in East Anglia, it is as old as horse-ploughing itself. Closely allied to the collecting of horse-shoes is that of blacksmiths' tools and many pubs display anvils and bellows. In some pubs, large bellows have been adapted to make very attractive occasional tables.

Inn Signs

'There is no form of original painting which is seen
by more people everyday than an Inn Sign.'
Richard Cobbold, Brewer

The collecting of inn signs is a fascinating hobby, although it is almost impossible actually to collect complete signs, except on occasions when they have been taken down from a pub which is to be closed or to have its name altered. However, with a polaroid camera, a collection of colour photographs can readily be obtained.

There is a large bibliography on this subject, but a few notes on the history of inn signs may prove interesting.

Pub signs have a very long pedigree, going back to the days of Pompeii, when pictorial signs were first used, one of the earliest being that of the chequer board, as I have mentioned previously. Furthermore, inn signs were a necessary form of identification in an age when most people were illiterate. Excavations at Pompeii have brought to light signs appropriate to various trades: a goat was the sign for a dairy, a mule the sign for a mill or baker, and two men carrying a large amphora of wine was the sign for the vintner.

The first inn sign noted in England was the ale stake—a long pole

A selection of inn signs taken from Larwood and Hotten's History of Signboards *(1866).*

BUSH.
(MS. of the 14th century.)

ROYAL OAK.
(Roxburghe Ballads, 1660.

ALE-POLE.
(Picture of Wouwverman, 17th cent.)

ELEPHANT AND CASTLE.
(Belle Sauvage Yard, circa 1668.)

BLACK JACK AND PEWTER PLATTER.
(Print by Schavelin, 1480.)

SPINNING SOW.
(France, 1520.)

CHESHIRE CHEESE.
(Modern sign, Aldermanbury, City.)

HAT AND BEAVER.
(Banks's Collection, 1750.)

BOAR'S HEAD
(Eastcheap.)

I AM THE ONLY
RUNNING FOOTMAN

RUNNING FOOTMAN.
(Charles Street, Berkeley Square, circa 1790.)

HARROW AND DOUBLET.
(Banks's Collection, 1700.)

GOOSE AND GRIDIRON.
(St Paul's Churchyard, circa 1800.)

protruding from the front of the house. Later, the simple stake was improved to include a bush and, still later, a sign. Early signs were simply painted on a board and suspended from the front of the house. Later they were hung from a sign post set up in the street. One of the largest surviving gallows signs, as these were called, is at The George in Stamford, Lincolnshire, and stretches right across the main street. In country places, some publicans even went so far as to erect a kind of triumphal arch in front of the house, from the centre of which was strung the sign board. A few of these still remain, notably at The Green Man and The Black Boy at Tutbury, near Burton-upon-Trent.

Eventually, regulations had to be brought in to restrict the distance which a sign could project across the highway as they had become a nuisance and a source of danger to passing horse-riders.

One of the most remarkable signboards ever erected was that at The White Hart at Scole in Norfolk. This was built in the year 1655 by James Peck, a merchant of Norwich, and is said to have cost £1,000, an absolute fortune in those days.

The choice of name for a public house can be of great commercial importance and Bickerdyke, in *The Curiosities of Ale and Beer*, tells of the landlord of The Magpie and Crown in Aldgate, a house famous for its ale, who was minded to discard the magpie from his sign and call the house simply The Crown. He did so with disastrous results, for his customers, who used to call his pub The Magpie, felt that The Crown was offering inferior ale. Custom fell off and the landlord died and the business came into the hands of a waiter of the house, named Renton, who put the magpie back on its old place on the signboard with such good effect that, on his death, the ex-waiter left behind him an estate of some £600,000, chiefly the product of The Magpie and Crown ale.

Among the artists of great repute who were commissioned to paint inn signs was, of course, Hogarth, who is said to have painted the famous 'A Man Loaded with Mischief, or Matrimony'. Richard Wilson RA painted the sign of The Loggerheads and this has given its name to a village near Mold in North Wales. The Royal Oak, painted by David Cox, is an inn sign at Betwys-y-Coed and, at Wargrave, on the Thames, near Henley, is the sign of The George and Dragon, painted by G.T. Leslie RA; the other side of this sign was painted by a Mr Hodgson ARA. It must be rare to have two such distinguished artists each painting one side of a sign.

Unskilful signboard painters were the subject of a royal proclamation by Good Queen Bess, who, with that figure of language which endeared her to the hearts of her faithful subjects, proved to be her father's daughter when she issued an order that 'portraits of herself by unskilful common painters should be knocked in pieces and cast into the fire'.

Modern inn-sign writers and painters have the advantage of being able to use the many new materials available. Patrick Murphy works in Burton upon Trent and produces his signs in relief-moulded fibreglass, which is very durable and, with occasional repainting, will last for many years. Most inn signs need repainting or retouching every seven to eight years because the wear and tear occasioned by wind and weather mean that the paintwork is bound to fade, in spite of the heavy coatings of varnish which are applied.

Another modern sign writer is John Cook, who operates from his Cheltenham studio and has assembled one of the best libraries on the fact and folklore of inn signs in the country. Another regional sign writer is the painter, Kate Aldous, who has produced many signs for the Ipswich brewers, Tollemache & Cobbold. Ken Walker is another traditional pub sign artist who works from Oldham Signs in Leeds, which is, in fact, owned by Allied Breweries. Like other sign writers, they go to immense trouble to research the history of the pub name and to reflect this in the eventual design.

Any serious collector of photographs of inn signs should endeavour to get hold of a copy of *The History of Signboards from the Earliest Times to the Present Day*, by Larwood and Hotten, first published in 1866. This immensely scholarly work includes over one hundred woodcuts of old inn signs which cover the history of sign boards from Roman days. Three of the woodcuts show that, even in mediaeval days, it was customary to have a sign outside the ale house to indicate its name; this was at a time when most people were illiterate. The indexing of the book is most interesting and the sign boards are grouped into chapters headed: 'Historic and Commemorative Signs', 'Heraldic and Emblematic Signs', 'Signs of Animals and Monsters', 'Birds and Fowls', 'Fish and Insects', 'Flowers, Trees, Herbs, etc', 'Biblical and Religious Signs', 'Saints, Martyrs, Etc', 'Dignities, Trades and Professions', 'The House and the Table', 'Dress; Plain and Ornamental', 'Geography and Topography', 'Humorous and Comic', 'Puns and Rebuses', 'Miscellaneous'.

This list could well form a basis for categorisation for any budding collector of pictures of inn signs who wishes to break them down under easily identifiable headings. The book traces the history of well over 2,000 different inn signs and names, both in Great Britain and on the continent of Europe.

Many pubs are associated with a particular historical or other character and the novice might well start by collecting inn signs of all pubs associated with, for example, Charles Dickens or Mr Pickwick, or of pubs associated with Admirals, such as Nelson and Codrington. Charles Dickens was, of course, a great enthusiast for the English tavern and a number of books have been published on the subject of the inns of Dickens and Pickwick.

Prints and Pictures

Of the prints of thousands of public houses, bars, coffee bars and taverns that exist or have existed over the centuries, it is pretty fair to say that, almost without exception, they have been painted, drawn, photographed or otherwise recorded in visual form, either by local artists or, in some cases, by famous illustrators.

The hobby of collecting prints of pubs is truly fascinating and they can be categorised in many ways, e.g. coaching inns, on a regional basis, by association with particular trades, military or naval victories, personalities. Indeed, the list of themes is almost endless. There are at present almost 67,000 licensed public houses in this country and, in addition, there are many more licensed premises, such as wine bars, restaurants, hotels and clubs.

The well-known Francis Frith collection has prints of photographs taken by Francis Frith between the years 1860 to 1890, when he visited almost every town and village in England in order to record the contemporary theme on glass negatives. Fortunately, these have been preserved and prints from them are now available and very clear and detailed they are too. In most small towns, there is an old well-established firm of photographers who may have stored negatives going back for two or three generations and these again can form a useful basis for research.

Public houses, both exteriors and interiors, have always formed an interesting subject for the artist and famous illustrators, such as Hogarth and Cruickshank, produced very large numbers of such pictures. A browse through any antiquarian book shop, or even the

Ye Olde Cheshire Cheese, Fleet Street. From a drawing by Arthur Moreland.

The George Inn.
Southwark.

Arthur
Moreland
1928

The George, Southwark. From a drawing by Arthur Moreland.

Some of the original prints by Rowlandson, Cruickshank and others on the wall of The Prince Regent, Marylebone High Street, London. This is one of the finest examples of a decorated Regency pub to be found. Michael Tierney, the 'Guv'nor', has been collecting for seventeen years.

ordinary bric-a-brac or junk shop, often produces an old volume in which are to be found woodcuts or engravings of old inns.

The search for prints of particular pubs, which may or may not still exist, can be pursued in the archives of town or county libraries. The Guildhall Library Print Department in London has a vast collection of originals and an excellent photocopying service, as does the library of the British Museum; and around Charing Cross Road area of London are numerous bookshops and sellers of prints where a rewarding hour or two may be spent thumbing through the stacks of old prints which are for sale. These seem remarkably inexpensive until one considers that, in the Victorian era, the printing of illustrated books was a phenomenal business. Public entertainment was not available to most of the populace but books were and they were very cheap and the libraries were available for all.

One of the great attractions about collecting prints is that they are

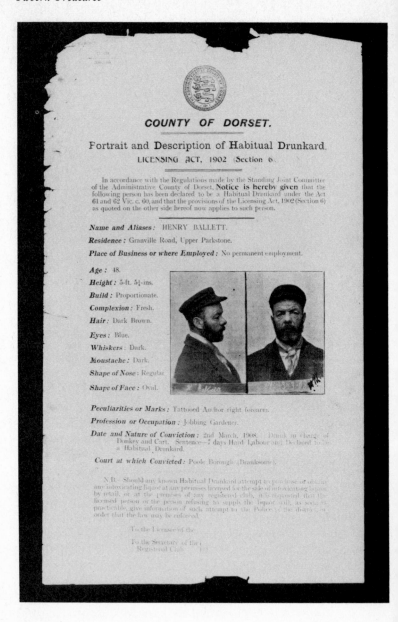

COUNTY OF DORSET.

Portrait and Description of Habitual Drunkard.

LICENSING ACT, 1902 (Section 6).

In accordance with the Regulations made by the Standing Joint Committee of the Administrative County of Dorset, **Notice is hereby given** that the following person has been declared to be a Habitual Drunkard under the Act 61 and 62 Vic. c. 60, and that the provisions of the Licensing Act, 1902 (Section 6) as quoted on the other side hereof now applies to such person.

Name and Aliases: HENRY BALLETT.

Residence: Granville Road, Upper Parkstone.

Place of Business or where Employed: No permanent employment.

Age: 48.

Height: 5-ft. 5¼-ins.

Build: Proportionate.

Complexion: Fresh.

Hair: Dark Brown.

Eyes: Blue.

Whiskers: Dark.

Moustache: Dark.

Shape of Nose: Regular.

Shape of Face: Oval.

Peculiarities or Marks: Tattooed Anchor right forearm.

Profession or Occupation: Jobbing Gardener.

Date and Nature of Conviction: 2nd March, 1908. Drunk in charge of Donkey and Cart. Sentence—7 days Hard Labour and Declared to be a Habitual Drunkard.

Court at which Convicted: Poole Borough (Branksome).

N.B.— Should any known Habitual Drunkard attempt to purchase or obtain any intoxicating liquor at any premises licensed for the sale of intoxicating liquor by retail, or at the premises of any registered club, it is requested that the licensed person or the person refusing to supply the liquor will, as soon as practicable, give information of such attempt to the Police of the district, in order that the law may be enforced.

To the Licensee of the

To the Secretary of the Registered Club

Portrait and description of an Habitual Drunkard as displayed in public houses according to the provisions of the Licensing Act 1902 (Section C).

easy to store and file and display as required and they do form a very informative history of the drinking habits of the nation over the years.

Bar notices can form an interesting addition to a collection of illustrations of pubs. Proclamations, both legal and advertising, have always been posted in bars as they were the centres in which people gathered in towns and villages throughout the country.

Some of the more interesting early ones have been reproduced and are available at souvenir and print shops, notably the calls for volunteers during World War 1, such as the picture of Lord Kitchener, pointing a finger at the observer with the words 'Your country needs YOU', and earlier posters endeavouring to recruit sailors for the Royal Navy in press-gang days.

Some of the more interesting notices are the legal announcements and one in particular is the Licensing Act of 1902 (6), which was printed by the National Trade Development Association and lists the various regulations applying to licensed premises.

At this time it was customary, when a person was convicted of being an habitual drunkard, to pin up a notice in the public house where he or she had been arrested and on this notice would be a profile and side view picture of the convicted person, rather like those ghastly photographs taken of prisoners today. This was posted as a warning that the person in question was banned from drinking in that pub and, in some cases, in any pub in the district for a period of up to three years. The recent new regulation, known as the 'Ban the Thug' Act, endeavours to emulate the regulations of eighty years ago and one wonders why the earlier law was ever allowed to lapse.

Souvenir Tea-Towels, Tee-Shirts and Sweat-Shirts

Every pub uses large quantities of tea-towels for drying and polishing glasses and there is at least one collector who has acquired a collection now numbering over 4,000 items. He is Tony Judkins, of 65 Liverpool Road, Luton, and his collection includes the many thousands of different advertising cloths printed by brewers, distillers, cigarette manufacturers and others. Almost every tourist centre and place of interest has printed tea-cloths to advertise their attractions and this is a fruitful field for those who wish to start collecting something which is not very expensive to acquire. Many of these cloths are produced in Irish linen and manufactured either in Eire or Ulster.

In this category, one might also include the current vogue for sweat-shirts and tee-shirts, emblazoned with advertising messages. These have proliferated now to the point where almost any slogan, be it political, religious or revolutionary, is to be seen proclaiming its message across the manly (or womanly) bosom of anyone bold enough to wear them. Any collection of such items associated with breweries and soft-drinks makers could become very large and might be broken down into regions, types of real ale, lagers or what you will. The problem of displaying them, however, might require the services of a veritable harem of girl friends to adequately show them off.

Trade Catalogues

A collection of brewery suppliers' catalogues makes fascinating reading and the Author's collection goes back to the latter part of the nineteenth century. In one catalogue, for example, there is a page illustrating three types of champagne-bottle stands. These held upside-down bottles of champagne with a tap fitted so that champagne could be served by the glass; it is interesting to note that, in 1900, a draught of champagne cost sixpence. One model in very good condition was sold at a London auction house for £550 quite recently. The same page lists various forms of champagne stopper and reclosures and, on the opposite page, no less than half a dozen lemon pressers and squeezers.

At that time, 'optics' as we know them had not appeared, not even the old 'Optic Pearl', a primitive form of tilting measure which looks very complicated from the illustration. Another page shows a range of money racks and change cabinets for dispensing both sovereigns and half sovereigns. Yet another page shows a choice of spittoons, match stands and counter and table bells.

The beautiful porcelain or cut-glass spirit urns and barrels illustrated in such catalogues make a very attractive form of collection. Prints of Victorian pubs show rows of these behind the bar (this was before the days of 'Optics') and they were topped up either by a spirit pump which drew the liquor up from the cellar or by gravity-feed from barrels which were stacked high behind the bar.

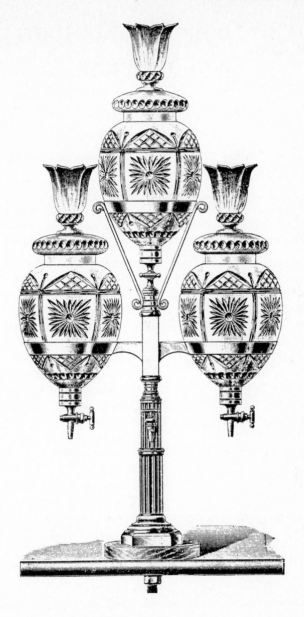

Special Triple Urn Stand. From the 1899 catalogue of T. Heath.

6 Some Notable Pubs and Museums

The Abundance of Pubs

The author, Sydney, writing in his book *England in the Eighteenth Century*, says:

> 'There was scarcely a public house in any respectable neighbourhood of the capital which had not its friends' club, its lottery club, its smoking club, its chanting club or its choir club in the parlour where the neighbouring shopkeepers regularly spent their evenings.'

In the reign of Edward I, however, there were only three taverns in London, one in Chepe, one in Wallbroke and one in Lombard Street. Even in the year 1552, the following list of the numbers of taverns allowed in the chief towns in Britain probably shows a much smaller number in proportion to the population than is seen at the present day. The numbers to be allowed were:

Bristol	6	London	40
Cambridge	4	Newcastle upon Tyne	4
Canterbury	4	Norwich	4
Chester	4	Salisbury	3
Colchester	3	Shrewsbury	3
Exeter	4	Southampton	3
Gloucester	4	Westminster	3
Hereford	3	Winchester	3
Hull	4	Worcester	3
Ipswich	3	York	8

These regulations have never been formally repealed. They were, however, very slackly enforced and soon became completely ignored. This is evidenced by a record of a petition presented in the year 1618 by the parishioners of St Mildred in London, which stated:

> 'Whereas the number of taverns has been limited to 40 and their places assigned, there were no less than 400 in the city alone. The Lord Mayor and Common Council are therefore directed to put some restraint on this enormous liberty of setting up taverns.'

Pubs Worth Visiting

'Who-e'er has travelled life's dull round,
Where'er his stages may have been,
May sigh to think he still has found,
The warmest welcome at an inn.'
(Shenstone)

There are some 67,000 licensed premises in Britain today and many
landlords have built up fascinating collections of memorabilia over
the years. Quite a number of them are happy to deal, swap or sell
their surplus items. The problem for the collector is finding which
ones are worth visiting. There is a whole range of guides which
provide useful information on finding collectors' pubs. The
Campaign for Real Ale Good Beer Guide is one such book, although
it does not necessarily list houses which specialise in breweriana. A
series of well-produced maps with guides to interesting public
houses is published by Better Pubs Ltd of Redcross House,
Crediton, Devon, and these cover most of the West Country and
southern counties. The National Trust owns a number of magnificent old inns and these are described in its book *Country House
Treasures*.

When visiting a pub for its collections, it is as well to check in
advance that the landlord who owns the collection is still in
residence. When a landlord moves to a new pub, he invariably takes
his collection with him and a long journey might otherwise be
wasted.

The Author has discovered many pubs with interesting collections over the past few years, all of them well worth visiting.

The Swan at Milton, near Repton, has an unusual collection of
getting on for one hundred different hats. They have been collected
by the licensee, Mike Whittaker, and his wife Rosemary. The hats
come from countries all over the world and customers on their
travels pick up unusual headgear to add to this collection.

There are a number of pubs which display collections of dolls
from around the world but one of the most impressive is at The
Riverside Inn near Christchurch, Dorset, where, in the spacious
rear bar, is a collection of over six hundred dolls—and upstairs
there are three hundred and eighty more waiting to be displayed!
The dolls come from countries all over the world and one
particularly interesting item is a special case displaying all the

English Queens, from Plantagenet days up to Queen Elizabeth I; the licensees have a special letter of authorisation from Buckingham Palace permitting them to show this range.

An outstanding pub collection can be seen at The Eagle public house at Watchfield, near Swindon in Wiltshire, where 1,500 key rings are displayed in the bar. This is not such an enormous collection when compared with an American who has acquired over 9,000 different key rings! A few years ago, there was a great craze in France for collecting car key rings and it was estimated at the time that, in the course of a year, the French had 'consumed' no less than fifteen key rings per adult head of population!

Key rings are obviously as old as keys themselves but modern collectors' items are often in the form of advertising signs of famous characters, such as Disneyland animals and the Muppets. There are also key rings with a practical use, incorporating nail clippers, pen knives and the signs of the zodiac, and they are produced and sold in pretty well every country in the world. Such a collection is not difficult to acquire and pubs which are located near airports or tourist centres and attract large numbers of tourists, both from Great Britain and overseas, are in a very favourable position to collect these from their many visitors. In Kent, Mr A.A. Dawkins, at The Elephant and Castle in Ashford, has a collection of well over one thousand but, as he says, 'Keeping them clean is like painting the Forth Bridge, it goes on all the time'.

Today, excellent reproductions of miners' or pit lamps are available which are in every way authentic but the true collector will want to find genuine lamps which have actually been used by a miner down a pit. There is one such collection at a pub appropriately called The Ironworks at Low Spennymoor, in County Durham, where the licensee, Dick Hockridge, recalls the days when he himself was down the pit. The oldest is a pair, manufactured by Ceag of Barnsley; lamps like this are now extremely difficult to find. There is also an original Davy lamp. Each lamp would have the miner's personal number engraved on a brass plate to serve as identification in the not-too-infrequent event of an accident.

More than one pub has a collection of chamber pots as a form of bar decoration but, at The White Hart at Aldeburgh, the licensee, Richard Bird, has made his pub a veritable shrine for sociologists whose special interest is sanitation! He now has nearly two hundred

Part of a collection of 2,000 cheese dishes at The Prince Regent, Marylebone High Street, London.

chamber pots, some of them dating back a hundred years or more. He also has several of the slipper type of bedpan, which he uses as giant ash-trays on his bar. When one recalls that, in days gone by, a chamber pot was as essential a piece of bedroom furniture as the bed itself, it is obvious that these were turned out in vast quantities and some of them were really beautifully decorated. Also one can find well-known naughty Victorian designs with an eye painted onto the base of the pot to stare up at the user!

These houses and others with collections worthy of mention, which have been visited by the author, are listed below. The list is very far from being exhaustive as there are literally thousands of such collections up and down the country.

Pubs with Notable Collections

Bedfordshire

THE CLAY PIPE, Leighton Buzzard: Clay pipes.

Clwyd
> THE BEE HOTEL, Rhyl (Carl Muller): Curios.

County Durham
> THE BRIDGE, Chester-le-Street (Jack Joplin): 1,000 model ships.
> THE IRONWORKS, Low Spennymoor (Dick Hockridge): Miner's lamps.

Derbyshire
> THE HARE AND GREYHOUND, Chesterfield (Fred Richards): Waiters' trays from the world.
> THE SWAN, Milton, Nr Repton: Hats from all over the world.

Devon
> THE ROYAL OAK, Ideford (Mrs Daphne Atkinson): 130 keys.

Dorset
> THE LORD NELSON, The Quay, Poole (Jim Kellaway): Souvenirs of shipwrecks from times of war and peace.
> THE RIVERSIDE INN, Tuckton, Nr Christchurch: 1,000 dolls, ships and other collections.
> THE WISE MAN, West Stafford, Nr Dorchester (Mr Hall): 200 pipes.

Glamorgan
> CAESAR'S ARMS, Creigiau: Memorabilia.

Gwent
> THE MOUNTAIN AIR INN, Tredegar (Bill Ingram): Saddlery collection.

Hampshire
> THE RED HOUSE INN, Whitchurch (Stewart Fee): Artifacts.

Kent
> THE ELEPHANT AND CASTLE, Ashford (A.A. Dawkins): 1,250 key rings.
> THE PRINCE ALBERT, Bexleyheath (John Mitchell): Brass, copper and nauticalia.
> THE RAILWAY TAVERN, Shincliffe (Michael Coulson): Antiques.
> THE SUSSEX ARMS, Tunbridge Wells (Dennis Lain): Beer engine.

London
> THE BUNCH OF GRAPES, Brompton Road, SW1: Victorian snob screens.
> THE CRICKETERS, Croydon: Collection of 600 weapons.

THE PRINCE REGENT, Marylebone High Street, W1 (Michael Tierney): Regency memorabilia and cheese dishes.

THE QUILL, Putney: 600 potties and earthenware hotwater bottles.

THE THREE TUNS, Blackheath, SE3: 200 Toby Jugs.

THE WATERMANS ARMS, Charlton, S.E.10: Nauticalia.

Lancashire

THE CROWN, Colne, E. Lancs (Walter Drabble): 100 Toby Jugs.

Lincolnshire

THE KINGS ARMS, Boston (Harry Seaman): Armoury.

Norfolk

THE LORD NELSON, Burnham Thorpe, Kings Lynn (Les Winter): Lord Nelson and Lady Hamilton relics.

Northamptonshire

THE BARTHOLOMEW ARMS, Blackesley (Sylvia and Tony Hackett): Breweriana.

THE RED LION, East Haddon: 27 oil lamps.

Salop

THE BRICKLAYERS, Nr Wem: Agricultural items.

THE CHURCH INN, Ludlow: Victorian beer engine.

THE GRANVILLE ARMS, New Handley, Telford (Arthur Simpson): A 'Sun' cork-lifter and other items.

THE THREE HORSESHOES, Alverley, Nr Bridgnorth: Roasting jacks and spit jacks.

Somerset

THE BUTCHERS ARMS, Cheddar (George Rogers): 100 Toby Jugs.

South Yorkshire

THE SILEY HOTEL, Shire Green, Sheffield (George Ellis): Arms and antiques.

Staffordshire

THE SHIP, Tamworth: A fine original 'Don' bench corkscrew.

Suffolk

THE BOOT, Dullingham, Newmarket (Mrs Green): Pottery boots.

THE WHITE HART, Aldeburgh (Richard Bird): 150 potties.

West Sussex

THE FOX AND HOUNDS, Singleton, Nr Chichester (Ralph Spillingsbury): A real bull's wooden leg.

West Yorkshire
> THE HARE AND HOUNDS, Rothwell, Nr Leeds (Tom Kelly): 600
> antiques.

Wiltshire
> THE EAGLE, Watchfield, Swindon: 1,500 key rings.

Museums Worth Visiting

Undoubtedly the best museum of brewing is that at Burton upon Trent, operated by the Bass Group. It really requires a full day to see over the whole of the very extensive premises with the outdoor exhibition of transport systems and the very well-conducted tour of the brewery itself. Needless to say, the visitor is not taken around the complete complex of buildings as this would take something like a week but in the two hours taken up by the tour, a great deal can be learned about both the history and the old and new techniques of brewing employed by this famous firm.

There is a smaller brewery museum at Stamford in Lincolnshire, which is situated in an old brewhouse in the town and this is well worth a visit if you should be in that part of the country.

In London, the Museum of Brewing was opening in 1980 in old brewery premises in Tower Bridge Road but unfortunately it had to close in 1981. It is hoped to reopen it in 1982 under the name of The Museum of Beer and the British Pub.

Other museums have specialist collections and a fine display of pub paraphernalia can be seen in the Brewery Section of the Watford Museum in Hertfordshire. Items can be purchased from their very extensive selection at David Plum's establishment at Grimsargh, near Preston in Lancashire (telephone Longridge 3351).

These and other museums mentioned previously are listed below:

> ACTON SCOTT WORKING FARM MUSEUM, Nr Church Stretton, Salop
> BASS MUSEUM, Burton upon Trent, West Midlands
> CITY AND COUNTY MUSEUM, Lincoln, Lincolnshire (Tokens)
> CITY OF PETERBOROUGH MUSEUM AND ART GALLERY, Peterborough, Cambridgeshire (Tokens)
> THE COUNTRY CENTRE, Clows Top, Nr Kidderminster, Worcestershire (Agricultural implements)
> GRANTHAM MUSEUM, Grantham, Lincolnshire (Tokens)

HARVEY'S OF BRISTOL WINE MUSEUM, Bristol, Avon

HOUSE OF PIPES MUSEUM, Steyning, Nr Bamber, West Sussex
  (Smokiana)

LONDON MUSEUM OF BREWING, Tower Bridge Road, London SE1
  (Closed 1981. To be reopened as The Museum of Beer and the
  British Pub in 1982)

MUSEUM OF CIDER, Hereford, Herefordshire

SPALDING GENTLEMEN'S SOCIETY MUSEUM, Spalding, Lincolnshire
  (Tokens)

STAMFORD BREWERY MUSEUM, Stamford, Lincolnshire

WATFORD MUSEUM (Brewery Section), Watford, Hertfordshire

Appendix
Commemorative Brews
since 1935

Silver Jubilee 1935

Special bottlings to commemorate the Silver Jubilee of HM King George, May 1935.

COMET ALE (JUBILEE)	Walker & Homfray's Ltd, Salford
JUBILEE ALE	Bentley & Shaw Ltd, Huddersfield
	Brickwood & Co. Ltd, Portsmouth
	Friary, Holroyd & Healey's Breweries Ltd, Guildford
	Ind Coope & Allsopp Ltd, Burton upon Trent
	Kenwood & Court Ltd, Hadlow
	T.D. Ridley & Sons (Brewers) Ltd, Chelmsford
	Tamplin & Sons Brewery (Brighton) Ltd, Brighton
	Thomson & Wotton Ltd, Ramsgate
JUBILEE PALE ALE	G.E. Cook & Sons Ltd, Halstead
SILVER JUBILEE BREW	Eldridge Pope & Co. Ltd, Dorchester
JUBILEE STOUT	Warwicks & Richardsons, Newark-on-Trent

Coronation 1937

Special bottlings to commemorate the Coronation of HM King George VI, May 1937.

BARLEY WINE CORONATION	Mann, Crossman & Paulin, Whitechapel

CORONATION	Bentley & Shaw, Huddersfield
CORONATION ALE	Wm Cooper & Co. Ltd, Southampton
	Fordham (E.K. & H.) Ltd, Ashwell
	Friary, Holroyd & Healey's Breweries Ltd, Guildford
	Greene King & Sons Ltd, Bury St Edmunds
	Kenward & Court Ltd, Hadlow
	Mappin's Masboro' Old Brewery Ltd, Rotherham
	Mauldon & Son Ltd, Ballingdon
	Morrell's Brewery Ltd, Oxford
	Tamplin & Sons Brewery (Brighton) Ltd, Brighton
	Tomson & Wotton Ltd, Ramsgate
	Peter Walker & Son Ltd, Liverpool
CORONATION BREW	Brickwood & Co. Ltd, Portsmouth
	Eldridge Pope & Co. Ltd, Dorchester
	Paine & Co. Ltd, St Neots
	H. & G. Simonds Ltd, Reading
CORONATION IPA	Lamb Brewery Ltd, Frome
CORONATION MILK STOUT	Tennent Bros Ltd, Sheffield
CORONATION STOUT	Bristol Brewery Georges & Co. Ltd, Bristol
CORONATION STRONG	John Smith's Tadcaster Brewery Ltd, Tadcaster
CROWN ALE	Elgood & Sons Ltd, Wisbech
EMPIRE ALE	Bentley's Old Brewery, Rotherham
SPECIAL CORONATION ALE	Rayment & Co. Ltd, Furneux Pelham

Coronation 1953

Special bottlings to commemorate the Coronation of HM Queen Elizabeth II, June 1953.

ANVIL BRAND PALE ALE CORONATION	Hydes Anvil Brewery Ltd, Manchester
CELEBRATION 53 SPECIAL	John Davenport & Sons Brewery Ltd, Birmingham
CORONATION	Hall & Woodhouse Ltd, Blandford Forum South London Brewery Ltd, London SE1
CORONATION ALE	Abington Brewery Co. Ltd, Northampton Adnams & Co. Ltd, Southwold James Aitken & Co. (Falkirk) Ltd, Falkirk Ballingall & Son Ltd, Dundee Charles Beasley Ltd, Plumstead Benskin's Watford Brewery Ltd, Watford Bentley's Yorkshire Breweries Ltd, Woodlesford Beverley Brothers Ltd, Wakefield Birkenhead Brewery Co. Ltd, Birkenhead W.H. Brakspear & Sons Ltd, Henley-on-Thames Brickwood & Co. Ltd, Portsmouth The Broadway Brewery Ltd, Shifnal Brutton, Mitchell, Toms Ltd, Yeovil Bushell, Watkins & Smith Ltd, Westerham Wm Butler & Co. Ltd, Wolverhampton Richard Clarke & Co. Ltd, Stockport Dales Brewery Ltd, Cambridge

CORONATION ALE (cont'd)

Daniell & Sons Breweries Ltd,
Colchester
James Deuchar Ltd, Montrose
Robert Deuchar Ltd, Edinburgh
Dutton's Blackburn Brewery Ltd,
Blackburn
Eldridge Pope & Co. Ltd,
Dorchester
Felinfoel Brewery Co. Ltd,
Llanelli
Sidney Fussel & Sons Ltd, Rode,
Nr Bath
Greene King & Sons Ltd, Bury
St Edmunds
John Groves & Sons Ltd,
Weymouth
Groves & Whitnal Ltd, Salford
Julia Hanson & Sons Ltd, Dudley
Harman's Uxbridge Brewery Ltd,
Uxbridge
G.S. Heath Ltd, Barrow
J.W. Hemingway Ltd, Leeds
Hey & Co. Ltd, Bradford
Holt Brothers Ltd, Burnham-on-
Sea
Hull Brewery Co. Ltd, Hull
Jennings Brothers Ltd,
Cockermouth
John Joule & Sons Ltd, Stone
Kemp Town Brewery (Brighton)
Ltd, Brighton
Matthews & Co., Gillingham,
Dorset
Mauldon & Sons Ltd, Ballingdon
McLennan & Urquhart Ltd,
Edinburgh
McMullen & Sons Ltd, Hertford
(Also for Fell & Bryant Ltd)
Mitchells & Butlers, Birmingham
Moors' & Robson's Breweries
Ltd, Hull
J. & J. Morison Ltd, Edinburgh
Morrell's Brewery Ltd, Oxford

CORONATION ALE (cont'd)

Wm Murray & Co. Ltd, Edinburgh
Nicholson & Sons Ltd, Maidenhead
J. Nimmo & Son Ltd, Castle Eden
Okell & Son Ltd, Douglas, I.O.M.
Paine & Co. Ltd, St Neots
Randalls Brewery Ltd, St Helier, Jersey
Rayment & Co. Ltd, Furneux Pelham
David Roberts & Sons Ltd, Aberystwyth
Shepherd Neame Ltd, Faversham
Shrewsbury & Wem Brewery Co. Ltd, Wem, Shrewsbury
H. & G. Simonds Ltd, Reading
John Smith's Tadcaster Brewery Ltd, Tadcaster
St Austell Brewery Co. Ltd, St Austell
Starkey, Knight & Ford Ltd, Bridgewater
Strong & Co. of Romsey Ltd, Romsey
Stroud Brewery Co. Ltd, Stroud
Taylor Walker & Co. Ltd, Limehouse
Tollemache's Breweries Ltd, Ipswich
Tomson & Wotton Ltd, Ramsgate
Vallances Brewery Ltd, Sidmouth
Peter Walker & Son Ltd, Liverpool
Webbs (Aberbeeg) Ltd, Abertillery
Welcome Brewery Co. Ltd, Oldham
Charles Wells Ltd, Bedford
Wells & Winch Ltd, Biggleswade
Whitworth Son & Nephew Ltd, Wath-on-Dearne

CORONATION ALE (cont'd)	Young & Co.'s Brewery Ltd, Wandsworth Robert Younger Ltd, Edinburgh
CORONATION ALE A1	Bents Brewery Ltd, Liverpool
CORONATION BEER	Devenish Weymouth Brewery Ltd, Weymouth Gibbs, Mew & Co. Ltd, Salisbury Yorkshire Clubs Brewery Ltd, Huntington
CORONATION BITTER	R. Whitaker & Sons Ltd
CORONATION BREW	Matthew Brown & Co., Blackburn Campbell Praed & Co. Ltd, Wellingborough Star Brewery Co. Ltd, Eastbourne Tuborg Ltd, Copenhagen, Denmark
CORONATION EXPORT ALE	Steel Coulson & Co. Ltd, Edinburgh
CORONATION HEAVY ALE	T. & J. Bernard Ltd, Edinburgh
CORONATION LIGHT ALE	T. & J. Bernard Ltd, Edinburgh
CORONATION OLD ALE	Wolverhampton & Dudley Breweries Ltd (Banks's), Wolverhampton
CORONATION PALE ALE	Cobbold & Co. Ltd, Ipswich
CORONATION REGAL	Leeds & Wakefield Breweries Ltd, Leeds
CORONATION STOUT	Bristol Breweries Georges & Co. Ltd, Bristol Sidney Fussell & Sons Ltd, Rode, Nr Bath E. Holden's Bottling Ltd, Dudley Wm Neesham Ltd, Ushaw Moor
CORONATION STRONG ALE	Gordon & Blair Ltd, Edinburgh H. Newnam & Sons Ltd, Stourbridge J.J. Young & Son Ltd, Portsmouth

CORONATION SWEET STOUT	Steel Coulson & Co. Ltd, Edinburgh
CORONATION VINTAGE ALE	Taylor Walker & Co. Ltd, Limehouse
CORONATION WREKIN ALE	Wrekin Brewery Co. Ltd, Wellington
CROWN ALE	Border Breweries (Wrexham) Ltd, Wrexham Lloyd & Yorath Ltd
CROWN IPA	Cobb & Co. (Brewers) Ltd, Margate
DOUBLE CROWN	P. Phipps & Co. Ltd. Northampton
ELIZABETHAN ALE	Bentley's Old Brewery (Rotherham) Ltd, Rotherham R.F. Case & Co. Ltd, Barrow-in-Furness Harvey & Son (Lewes) Ltd, Lewes
ELY CORONATION ALE	East Anglian Breweries Ltd, Ely Ely Brewery Co. Ltd, Cardiff
53 ALE	Dryborough & Co. Ltd, Edinburgh
INDIA PALE ALE	Wm McEwan & Co. Ltd, Edinburgh
KING'S ALE (CORONATION)	Matthew Brown & Co., Blackburn
LB BITTER	Matthew Brown & Co., Blackburn
LOYALTY ALE	Burtonwood Brewery Co. (Forshaws) Ltd, Burtonwood
MONARCH	Marston, Thompson & Evershed Ltd, Burton upon Trent Morland & Co. Ltd, Abingdon
MONARCH ALE DARK STRONG	Marston, Thompson & Evershed, Burton upon Trent
OAKWELL ROYAL	Barnsley Brewery Co. Ltd, Barnsley

OLD BROWN CORONATION ALE	Samuel Webster & Sons Ltd, Halifax
PALE ALE THE FAMILY ANVIL	Hydes Anvil Brewery Ltd, Manchester
QUEEN'S ALE	Alton Court Brewery Co. Ltd, Ross-on-Wye Castletown Brewery Ltd, Castletown, I.O.M. Catterall & Swarbrick's Brewery Ltd, Blackpool Fremlins Ltd, Maidstone Lancashire Clubs Brewery Ltd, Barrowford Scarborough & Whitby Breweries Ltd, Scarborough Tamplin & Sons Brewery (Brighton) Ltd, Brighton Wadworth & Co Ltd, Devizes
RUSSIAN IMPERIAL STOUT	Barclay, Perkins & Co. Ltd, Southwark
SILVER CROWN ALE	Evan Evans Bevan Ltd, Neath
SOVEREIGN	Friary, Holroyd & Healey's Breweries Ltd, Guildford
STRONG ALE	Thomas Usher and Son Ltd, Edinburgh
TRIPLE CROWN	Usher's Wiltshire Brewery Ltd, Trowbridge
UNICORN CORONATION ALE	Frederic Robinson Ltd, Stockport Arthur Guinness Son & Co. Ltd, Park Royal, London. (A specially moulded bottle)

Silver Jubilee 1977 and Other Commemorative Ales, Beers and Lagers

Special brews and bottlings mainly to commemorate the Silver Jubilee of HM Queen Elizabeth II, July 1977. The following list contains details of all beers believed to have been brewed during 1977 of a commemorative nature. Only the products of 'Brewers for Sale' have been included.

CELEBRATION ALE	275 ml	Morrel's Brewery Ltd, Oxford
	180 ml	Oldham Brewery Co. Ltd, Oldham
CORONATION BREW	180 ml	Eldridge Pope & Co. Ltd, Dorchester
CROSS KEYS JUBILEE ALE	180 ml	Cross Keys PH, Pulloxhill, Bedfordshire
CROWN ALE	275 ml	J.W. Cameron & Co. Ltd, Hartlepool
ELIZABETHAN ALE	170 ml	Harvey & Son (Lewes) Ltd, Lewes
JUBILATION	(Draught)	Three Tuns, Bishop's Castle (Home brew)
JUBILEE ALE	274 ml	L.C. Arkell
	170 ml	Matthew Brown & Co., Blackburn
	275 ml	G.E. Cook & Sons Ltd, Halstead
	275 ml	Greene King & Sons Ltd, Bury St Edmunds
	275 ml	Guernsey Brewery Co. (1920) Ltd, St Peter Port
	275 ml	Hook Norton Brewery Co. Ltd, Hook Norton (Labels bearing the name OLD BILL CELEBRATION ALE were printed but no beer was bottled by the brewery under that label.)
	180 ml	King & Barnes Ltd, Horsham
	275 ml	R.W. Randall Ltd, St Peter Port, Guernsey
	275 ml	T.D. Ridley & Sons (Brewers) Ltd, Chelmsford

JUBILEE ALE (cont'd)	275 ml	St Austell Brewery Co. Ltd, St Austell
	275 ml	James Shipstone & Sons Ltd, Nottingham
JUBILEE LAGER	275 ml	Grunhalle Lager International Ltd
	275 ml	Northern Clubs' Federation Breweries Ltd, Hull
JUBILEE MALT ALE	275 ml	Jennings Brothers Ltd, Cockermouth
JUBILEE PALE ALE	180 ml	Charles Wells Ltd, Bedford
JUBILEE REAL ALE	275 ml	York Brewery (John Boothroyd), York
JUBILEE STRONG ALE	275 ml	Home Brewery Co. Ltd, Daybrook
KINGSDOWN ALE	275 ml	J. Arkell & Sons Ltd, Swindon
MARY ANN JUBILEE DIET LAGER	275 ml	Ann Street Brewery Co. Ltd, St. Helier, Jersey
MONARCH BARLEY WINE	170 ml	Morland & Co. Ltd, Abingdon
OLD ANSTY JUBILEE ALE	275 ml	The Fox PH, Ansty, Dorset
PALE ALE SPECIAL LABEL	275 ml	Hydes Anvil Brewery Ltd, Manchester
	550 ml	Hydes Anvil Brewery Ltd, Manchester
	730 ml	Hydes Anvil Brewery Ltd, Manchester
QUEEN'S ALE	275 ml	Wadworth & Co. Ltd, Devizes
RANDALL'S JUBILEE ALE	275 ml	Randall's Brewery Ltd, St. Helier, Jersey
REGAL ALE	275 ml	Belhaven Brewery Co. Ltd, Dunbar
	180 ml	Devenish Redruth Brewery Ltd, Redruth
ROYAL ALE	275 ml	Adnams & Co. Ltd, Southwold

ROYAL WREXHAM BARLEY WINE 170 ml		Border Breweries (Wrexham) Ltd, Wrexham
SILVER CELEBRATION	275 ml	Fuller, Smith & Turner Ltd, Chiswick
	275 ml	Okell & Son Ltd, Douglas, I.O.M.
SILVER CROWN	275 ml	Marston, Thompson & Evershed Ltd, Burton upon Trent
SILVER JUBILEE ALE	275 ml	Courage Ltd (Two labels, one without '1977')
	275 ml	Everards Brewery Ltd, Burton upon Trent
	180 ml	George Gale & Co. Ltd, Horndean
	275 ml	George Gale & Co. Ltd, Horndean (Not sold)
	175 ml	Paine & Co. Ltd, St Neots
	275 ml	Shepherd Neame Ltd, Faversham
	330 ml	Whitbread & Co. Ltd
SILVER JUBILEE GUINNESS		Arthur Guinness Son & Co. Ltd, Park Royal, London (Not sold. Two neck-straps: an English or a Scottish crown)
SILVER JUBILEE STRONG ALE	275 ml	Ansells Brewery Ltd, Birmingham
	275 ml	Ind Coope Ltd
SILVER JUBILEE STRONG PALE ALE	275 ml	Joshua Tetley & Son Ltd, Leeds
SILVER PALE ALE	275 ml	Norwich Brewery Ltd, Norwich
SILVER SOVEREIGN	275 ml	Young & Co.'s Brewery Ltd, Wandsworth
SOVEREIGN ALE	275 ml	Elgood & Sons Ltd, Wisbech
SPECIAL JUBILEE ALE	275 ml	Wolverhampton & Dudley Breweries Ltd (Banks's), Wolverhampton

Miscellaneous

Brewed for bottling in 1979	Bass Ltd
Draught beer	Gibbs, Mew & Co. Ltd, Salisbury
A special beer. Not sold.	Greenall Whitley & Co. Ltd, Warrington
Draught beer	Hartleys (Ulverston) Ltd, Ulverston
Draught beer. A few dozen bottled but not sold.	J.P.S. Breweries Ltd
Draught lager	J.W. Lees & Co., Manchester
Limited edition lager 330 ml	Skol (Allied Breweries UK) Ltd
Draught beer	Tollemache & Cobbold Breweries Ltd (Tolly Cobbold), Ipswich
Special label 275 ml	Traquair House, Innerleithan

Special Brews in 1977 (Not including the Silver Jubilee)

Bass Ltd	BASS 200 to celebrate the bicentenary of the company.
Bass Ltd	HODGES CENTENARY ALE
Courage Ltd	Star bicentenary
Everards Brewery Ltd, Burton upon Trent	Robert Morton Ltd
Hall Woodhouse Ltd, Blandford Forum	Bicentenary of the company.
Marston, Thompson & Evershead, Burton upon Trent	Darley 100 years of print (OWD ROGER).
Scottish & Newcastle	Golden Jubilee of Newcastle Brown Ale.
J.P. Simpkiss & Son Ltd, Brierly Hill	EXHIBITION ALE for Newey & Eyres.
Tollemache & Cobbold Breweries Ltd (Tolly Cobbold), Ipswich	CARDINAL JUBILEE ALE
Charles Wells Ltd, Bedford	CROSS KEYS OKTOBERFEST ALE

Bass Ltd	Bass' SILVER JUBILEE ALE mashed for bottling in 1978

Special Brews in 1978

Bass Ltd	Bottling of SILVER JUBILEE ALE. Bottles to be available for charity. Apply to the Bass Museum, Burton upon Trent.
Bass Ltd	4,800 ½-pint bottles of strong export ale bottled to commemorate the Centenary of Burton upon Trent. Sold for £1 each from May 13–22.
Bass Ltd	HRH Princess Anne mashed a special beer on June 6. This was for bottling in 1979.
Boddingtons Breweries Ltd, Manchester	A special beer brewed and bottled to commemorate the company's Bicentenary.
Eldridge Pope & Co. Ltd, Dorchester	A barley wine with an o.g. of 1085° called SHERBOURNE ABBEY ALE. Profits from its sale to be donated to the Abbey repair fund.
Elgood & Sons Ltd, Wisbech	A special ale to commemorate the company's Centenary.
Everards Brewery Ltd, Burton upon Trent	CELEBRATION ALE FOR Almasco.
Felinfoel Brewery Co. Ltd, Llanelli	A special brew to commemorate the company's Centenary
Home Brewery Ltd	A special brew to commemorate the company's Centenary.
J.W. Lees & Co., Manchester	A special brew to commemorate the company's 150 years.
Manns Northampton Brewery Co. Ltd, Northampton	NORCON ALE bottled for the Northampton Junior Chamber Conference, September 7–9.

Paine & Co. Ltd, St Neots	A special ale bottled for the visit of seventy-five New Zealand Squadron RAF Old Comrades, August 26.
Paine & Co. Ltd, St Neots, Thos Wethered & Sons Ltd, Marlow, and Whitbread & Co. Ltd	PULLOXHILL CHURCH ALE. The first two brewers bottled in 9.68 fl. oz. and Whitbreads in 6 fl. oz. bottles. Sold in aid of church funds.
Watney Mann & Truman Brewers Ltd	ST GEORGE'S ALE. Specially bottled for St George's Day.
Samuel Webster & Sons Ltd, Halifax	Golden Jubilee of GREEN LABEL Pale Ale.
Young & Co.'s Brewery Ltd, Wandsworth	HEAVY HORSES for the promoters of a Jethro Tull gramophone record.

Special Brews in 1979

The following beers have been reported to The Brewers' Society:

J. Arkell & Son Ltd, Swindon	125th anniversary of Paddington Station. On sale in selected ex-Great Western Railway bars in March.
Bass Ltd	Bottling of PRINCESS ALE mashed in 1978.
Bass Mitchells & Butlers Ltd, Birmingham	Centenary of Mitchells & Butlers, April.
W.H. Brakspear & Sons Ltd, Henley-on-Thames	Bicentenary, April.
Courage Ltd	Closing of H. & G. Simonds Brewery/Opening of The Berkshire Brewery, late April.
Eldridge Pope & Co. Ltd, Dorchester	REMEMBRANCE ALE in aid of the Earl Haig Fund. Available through company outlets. First 100,000 bottles are numbered. 275 ml bottles retailing at approx. 27p.

Ind Coope Burton Brewery Ltd, Burton upon Trent	FOUNDATION ALE 1979 for Burton Junior Chamber. (Contact Mr R. Sutton: 0283 217905 (office) or 0283 216225 (home); Mrs McGlynn: 0283 45320 Extension 2734 (office) or 0283 45273 (home). 10,000 bottles @ £1 + p. & p.) REGATTA ALE for Burton upon Trent Riverside Show, July 1979.
Ind Coope Scotland Ltd	CHARTER 650. Lager to celebrate the 650th anniversary of the Charter of Edinburgh.
Morland & Co. Ltd, Abingdon	OLD SPECKLED HEN. To celebrate 50 years association of MG with Abingdon, Berks.
Okell & Sons Ltd, Douglas	Millenium of Tynwald, 30 March 1979.
Paine & Co. Ltd, St Neots	WM PENN ALE, 7 July 1979.
G. Ruddle & Co. Ltd, Oakham	Special canning for 100 years of BR catering.
Traquair House, Innerleithen	100th brew from the estate brewery.
Frederick Wing	WINGS CELEBRATION ALE. 200th Derby, 6 June 1979. A home brew (not for sale but for exchange) by F. Wing. Esq., 11 Oxford Road, Guildford, Surrey.

Royal Wedding Ales 1981

A consolidated list of special beers brewed or bottled to commemorate the wedding of HRH Prince Charles and Lady Diana Spencer, June 1981. Sources: The Brewers' Society; The Labologists' Society; *What's Brewing* and the general public. Lower case in the first column indicates that the beer name is not known.

ALBERT ALE	275 ml	Albert Arms PH, Esher, Surrey. Brewed by Bourne Valley Brewery Ltd, Andover. Bottled by

ALBERT ALE (cont'd)		Gibbs, Mew & Co. Ltd, Salisbury.
BANDWAGON	330 ml	White Hart PH, Newhaven, Sussex (50 bottles only)
BANKS'S SPECIAL BREW	275 ml	Wolverhampton & Dudley Breweries Ltd (Banks's), Wolverhampton
BELLE CROWN	275 ml	Bourne Valley Brewery Ltd, Andover. Fired-on label.
BLUEBEARD ROYAL WEDDING SPECIAL ALE 1981	275 ml	(See also—NUPTIAL NIP) Golden Hind PH, Hastings, Sussex. Brewed by Martlet Brewery, Eastbourne.
Brewers' Arms	275 ml	Brewers' Arms PH, Vines Cross, Sussex. Brewed by Harvey & Son (Lewes) Ltd, Lewes.
BRIDAL ALE	250 ml	Godson, Freeman & Wilmot Ltd, London E3
BRIDAL PORTER	Draught	Canterbury Brewery, Canterbury
CELEBRATION ALE	275 ml	Jennings Brothers Ltd, Cockermouth
	275 ml	Maclay & Co. Ltd, Alloa Northampton Beer Agency, Brewed by Paine & Co. Ltd, St Neots
	275 ml	R.W. Randall Ltd, Guernsey
	275 ml	Ushers Brewery Ltd, Trowbridge. (Two labels: White & Blue, Silver and Blue)
CELEBRATION BREW	275 ml	Fuller, Smith & Turner Ltd, Chiswick
	275 ml	Home Brewery Co. Ltd, Nottingham
	354 ml	Whitbread & Co. Ltd, London
CELEBRATION LAGER	275 ml	Young & Co.'s Brewery Ltd, London
CELEBRATION ROYALE	180 ml	King & Barnes Ltd, Horsham

157

CELEBRATION ROYALE (cont'd) 250 ml	King & Barnes Ltd, Horsham. (For the Italian market.)
CELEBRATION SPECIAL 275 ml	Ann Street Brewery Co. Ltd, St. Helier, Jersey
CEREMONIAL ALE 275 ml	Courage Ltd, London
CHAD Draught	Ironbridge Brewery, East London
CHARLES & DIANA 264 ml	Penrhos Court, Kington
CHARLES CELEBRATION Draught	Old Chidham Brewery Ltd, Chichester
CHARLES CELEBRATION BREW 275 ml	Old Chidham Brewery Ltd, Chichester
Downings Draught	Fox & Hounds PH, Stottesdon
DUKE OF CORNWALLS NUPTIAL ALE Draught	Paradise Brewery, Hayle (Bottle and neck labels exist)
Falkland Arms	Falkland Arms PH, Great Tew. Brewed by Hook Norton Brewery Co. Ltd, Hook Norton
GOLIATH CELEBRATION BEER 500 ml	Amateur Winemakers, Middlesborough
GREYHOUND 275 ml	Elgood & Sons Ltd, Wisbech
GUESS WHO'S ROYAL WEDDING ALE 81 Draught $19\frac{1}{4}$ fl. oz.	Goose Eye Brewery, Keighley. Bottled by Legendary Yorkshire Heroes Ltd
Holdens Draught	Holden's Brewery Ltd, Woodsetton
HONEST JOHN ROYAL BREW 275 ml	Honest John PH, Chatteris. Brewed by Greene King Biggleswade Ltd, Biggleswade
HOPS & GRAPES COMMEMORATIVE ALE 275 ml	Hops & Grapes O/L, Brighton. Brewed by Martlet Brewery, Eastbourne
IECHYD DA 275 ml	Gwynedd Brewery, Gaerwen Industrial Estate, Anglesey
IND COOPE STRONG LAGER 330 ml	Wrexham Lager Beer Co. Ltd, Wrexham

Kelly's Draught		Kelly's Real Ale Brewery, Hurworth
Lea Gate Inn	275 ml	Lea Gate Inn, Coningsby. Brewed by Paine & Co. Ltd, St Neots
NUPTIAL NIP	180 ml	Golden Hind PH, Hastings, Sussex. Brewed by Martlet Brewery, Eastbourne (See also BLUEBEARD ROYAL WEDDING SPECIAL)
NUPTIALE Draught		Hardington Brewery, Hardington
OWN ALE ROYAL WEDDING SPECIAL BREW 1981	275 ml	Miners Arms Restaurant, Priddy, Somerset
PRINCE OF ALES Draught & bottled		Blue Anchor, Helston
	264 ml	Bruce's Brewery, London SE1
	275 ml	T. & R. Theakston Ltd, Masham
PRINCE OF WALES SPECIAL BREW		Carlsberg Ltd, Northampton
PRINCES ALE	275 ml	Adnams & Co. Ltd, Southwold
	275 ml	S.A. Brain & Co. Ltd, Cardiff
	275 ml can	Felinfoel Brewery Co. Ltd, Llanelli
PRINCES PREFERENCE	275 ml	Chiltern Brewery
PRINCESS ALE	275 ml	Belhaven Brewery Co. Ltd, Dunbar
QUEENS HEAD BITTER	275 ml	Queens Head Hotel, Hawkhurst, Kent
RIGHT ROYAL ALE Draught & bottled		The Wood Brewery, Wistanstow
ROYAL ALE	275 ml	Everards Brewery Ltd, Leicester
	9.68 fl. oz.	Guernsey Brewery Co. (1920) Ltd, St Peter Port
	180 ml	Oldham Brewery Co. Ltd, Oldham
ROYAL BREW	275 ml	Litchborough Brewing Co. Ltd, Litchborough (3,000 bottles)

ROYAL BREW EXTRA STRONG LAGER	275 ml	Bass Ltd, London. Brewed in Sheffield
ROYAL CELEBRATION ALE	275 ml	North Country Breweries Ltd, Hull
	275 ml	Frederic Robinson Ltd, Stockport
	275 ml	Watneys London Ltd, Mortlake
ROYAL DELPH ALE	Draught	Daniel Batham & Son Ltd, Brierley Hill
ROYALE BREW	275 ml	Hawthorne Brewery, Gloucester. (Two labels)
ROYALE FLUSH	Draught & 35 bottles	Turners Golden Star Brewery, Norwich
ROYAL HERITAGE	275 ml	Gibbs, Mew & Co. Ltd, Salisbury
ROYAL HONEYMOON ALE		New Inn, Waterley Bottom (200 bottles)
ROYAL LOVE POTION	275 ml	Phillips Brewing Co., Marsh Gibbon (500 bottles)
	550 ml	Phillips Brewing Co., Marsh Gibbon (123 bottles)
ROYAL MATCH	264 ml	Ringwood Brewery, Ringwood
ROYAL PILSENER LAGER BEER	275 ml	Marston, Thompson & Evershed Ltd, Burton upon Trent
ROYAL RECEPTION STRONG ALE	275 ml	Berni Inns. Brewed by Watney Mann & Truman Brewers Ltd.
ROYAL RICHMOND	275 ml	Richmond Arms PH, West Ashling. Brewed by Ballards Brewery
ROYAL TOAST	275 ml	Harvey & Son (Lewes) Ltd, Lewes
	180 ml	Wheatsheaf PH, St Leonards. Brewed by Charrington & Co. Ltd, London
ROYAL WEDDING	275 ml	The Fox PH, Ansty. Brewed by Hall & Woodhouse, Blandford Forum
	275 ml	Hall & Woodhouse Ltd, Blandford Forum

ROYAL WEDDING (cont'd)

275 ml	Morland & Co. Ltd, Abingdon

ROYAL WEDDING ALE

275 ml	J. Arkell & Sons Ltd, Swindon, Wilts
275 ml	Buckley's Brewery Ltd, Llanelli
275 ml	J.W. Cameron & Co. Ltd, Hartlepool
275 ml	Crown PH, Little Missenden. Brewed by Paine & Co. Ltd, St Neots
275 ml	George Gale & Co. Ltd, Horndean
275 ml	Greene King & Sons Ltd, Bury St Edmunds
275 ml	Higsons Brewery Ltd, Liverpool
275 ml	Hook Norton Brewery Ltd, Hook Norton Minchery Farm Country Club, Oxford. Brewed by Hook Norton Brewery Ltd, Hook Norton
275 ml	Morrell's Brewery Ltd, Oxford
170 ml	Okell & Son Ltd, Douglas, I.O.M.
275 ml	Penruddocke Arms PH, Dinton. Brewed by Wadworth & Co. Ltd, Devizes (A few 180 ml)
275 ml	Pheasant Brewery, Gestingthorpe
275 ml	St Austell Brewery Ltd, St Austell
275 ml	Shepherd Neame Ltd, Faversham
275 ml	Swan & Brewer PH, Great Kimble. Brewed by Morrell's Brewery Ltd, Oxford
275 ml	Tollemache & Cobbold Breweries Ltd, Ipswich
275 ml	Two Brewers O/L. Brewed by Jennings Brothers Ltd, Cockermouth

ROYAL WEDDING BREW

	Broughton Brewery, Nr Biggar
Draught	Yates & Jackson Ltd, Lancaster
Draught	(Polypin label issued)
550 ml	Yates & Jackson Ltd, Lancaster.

ROYAL WEDDING BREW (cont'd)		Draught beer bottled by Legendary Yorkshire Heroes (Fifty 1-pint bottles)
ROYAL WEDDING COLLECTORS ALE	275 ml	Hop Inn, Reading. Brewed by Gibbs, Mew & Co. Ltd, Salisbury
ROYAL WEDDING SPECIAL ALE	275 ml	Village Blacksmith O/L, Woolwich. Brewed by Tisbury Brewery Co., Tisbury
SALISBURY ARMS COMMEMORATIVE ALE	275 ml	Salisbury Arms PH, Southampton. Brewed by Marston, Thompson & Evershed Ltd, Burton upon Trent
SALUTATION Draught and bottled Ship Inn	275 ml	Three Tuns Brewery, Bishop's Castle Ship Inn, Chatteris. Brewed by Paine & Co. Ltd, St Neots
SPECIAL TRADITIONAL BITTER	440 ml	J.W. Lees & Co., Manchester
STRONG PORTER	440 ml	Samuel Smith Old Brewery (Tadcaster) Ltd, Tadcaster
Sussex		Sussex Brewery, Edburton. 100 bottles by Hops & Grapes PH, Brighton
THE 'NOT THE ROYAL WEDDING ALE'	275 ml	The Goat PH, St Albans. Brewed by the Victoria Brewery, Ware.
	550 ml	The Goat PH, St Albans. Brewed by the Victoria Brewery, Ware. (60 bottles only)
THE ROYAL WEDDING ALE	354 ml	John Smith's Tadcaster Brewery Ltd, Tadcaster
TIPPLE	275 ml	Prince of Wales PH, Hammer Vale. Brewed by George Gale & Co. Ltd, Horndean
V.S.P.	275 ml	Wilsons Brewery Ltd, Manchester
WEDDING ALE	275 ml	Devenish Weymouth Brewery Ltd, Weymouth
	275 ml	John Thompson PH. Brewed by

WEDDING ALE (cont'd)		George Gale & Co. Ltd, Horndean
	275 ml	Joshua Tetley & Son Ltd, Leeds
	275 ml	Daniel Thwaites & Co. Ltd, Blackburn
	275 ml	Charles Wells Ltd, Bedford
WEDDING BREW Draught		J.P. Simpkiss & Son Ltd, Brierley Hill
WEDDING DAY ALE	275 ml	Victoria Brewery, Ware (150 bottles)
WEDDING DAY SPECIAL ALE	275 ml	Dolphin Brewery, Poole
WELLINGTON SALUTE		
	180 ml	Duke of Wellington PH, Hastings
	275 ml	Duke of Wellington PH, Hastings
	550 ml	Duke of Wellington PH, Hastings (12 bottles only)
YOUNG ROWLEY	275 ml	Paine & Co. Ltd, St Neots
	330 ml	Paine & Co. Ltd, St Neots (For the Italian market.)

Birth of HRH Prince William 1982

A number of the smaller independent brewers have produced a brew to commemorate the birth of Prince William but details of the labelling have still to be announced. The brewers are:

Gibbs, Mew, Dorchester/Salisbury
Paine & Co. Ltd, St Neots
Guernsey Brewery Co. (1920) Ltd, St Peter Port
The Ironbridge Tavern (P.H.), London

However, one major brewer has marketed a special pack:

ROYAL ALE	A strong ale especially brewed by Truman, Hanbury and Buxton to celebrate the birth of the first child to the Prince and Princess of Wales 1982.

Information supplied by courtesy of The Brewers' Society, Portman Square, London W1

Societies

Beer Can Collectors of America,
747 Merus Court, Fenton, MO
63026, USA

The Brewers' Society,
Portman Square, London W1

Brewery History Society,
Membership Secretary: Colin White, Flat 6,
Police Station, Margate Road, Guildford, Surrey

British Beer Can Collectors' Society,
Hon. Sec. Martin White, 74 Bleaswood Road,
Oxenholme, Kendal, Cumbria

British Beer Mat Collectors' Society,
Hon. Sec. Brian West, 10 Coombe Hill Crescent,
Thame, Oxfordshire

Campaign For Real Ale, 34 Alma Road,
St. Albans, Hertfordshire AL1 3BW

Cast Iron Seat Collectors' Association,
c/o Terry Keegan, The Oxleys, Clows Top,
Nr Kidderminster, Worcestershire

Cast Iron Seat Collectors' Association of
America,
c/o Carol Scheenan, Route 1, Rushville, Nebraska 69360
Box 48

Eastern Coast Breweriana Association,
30201 Royalview Drive, Willowick, OH 44094,
USA

Labologist's Society,
Membership Secretary: Roy Dennison, 24 Pennypiece,
Goring-on-Thames, Reading, Berkshire

Mini Bottle Club, Hon. Sec. Mrs Ivy Grant,
'Seas-gu-Daighean', Lynden Lane,
Stonegate, Nr Wadhurst, Sussex

Music Box Society of Great Britain,
40 Station Approach, Hayes, Bromley, Kent

164

Miniature Bottles (Trade Only),
Malcolm Cowen Ltd., Britannia Way,
Coronation Road, London NW10

National Association of Breweriana Advertising,
c/o Gordon B. Dean, Wilson Memorial Drive,
Chassel, MI 49916, USA

National Horsebrass Society, c/o D.R. Green,
Orchard End, Farm Road, Sutton, Surrey

Pewter Society, Sec. M.F. Brazell,
'Claremont', 12 Whittlebury Court,
Whittlebury, Towcester,
Northamptonshire NN12 BXQ

Royal Doulton International Collectors' Club,
5 Egmont House, 116 Shaftesbury Avenue,
London W1

Society for the Preservation of Beer from the Wood,
c/o Ye Olde Watling PH, Watling Street,
London EC4.

Bibliography

Books are listed either under General Interest or under chapter headings.

General Interest

Aldin, C. (1921) *Old Inns* Eyre & Spottiswoode Ltd

Barclay, Perkins & Co. Ltd. (1951) *Three Centuries. The Story of our Ancient Brewery* Harley Publishing Co. Ltd

Barnard, A. (1889/91) *The Noted Breweries of Great Britain and Ireland* Volumes 1–4

Bickerdyke, J. (1899) *The Curiosities of Ale & Beer* Reprinted 1965 by Spring Books, London

Hackwood, F.W. (1909) *Inns, Ales and Drinking Customs of Old England* Fisher Unwin, London

Heywood, T. (1635) *Philocothonista or the Drunkard Opened, Dissected and Anatomised*

Juniper, W. (1933) *The True Drunkard's Delight* Unicorn Press, London

McWhirter, N.D., ed. (1982) *Guinness Book of Records* Guinness Superlatives, Enfield

Monkton, H.A. (1966) *History of English Ale and Beer*

Owen, C.C. (1978) *The Development of Industry in Burton upon Trent* Phillimore Ltd, Chichester

Platter, Thomas (1599) *Travels in England*

Stuart, D. (1975) *History of Burton on Trent* Parts I and II The Charter Trustees of Burton on Trent

Thomason, Sir Edward (1845) *Memoirs During Half a Century* Volumes 1 and 2 Longmans, Brown, Green and Longman, London

Whitbread (1945–1950) *1. Whitbread's Brewery; 2. Your Local; 3. Inn-Signia; 4. The Brewer's Art; 5 Whitbread Craftsmen; 6. Inns of Kent; 7. Inns of Sport; 8. Receipts & Relishes; 9. Your Club; 10. Inn Crafts and Furnishings* Whitbread's Brewery, London

Behind the Bar

Cotterell, H.H. (1968) *Old Pewter: Its Makers and Marks* Batsford, London (New edition)

Dolphin R. (1977) *International Book of Beer Can Collecting* Hamlyn, London

Fletcher, E. (1975) *International Bottle Collectors' Guide* Blandford Press, Poole

Fletcher, E. (1976) *Non-Dating Price Guide to Bottles, Pipes and Dolls' Heads* Blandford Press, Poole
Fletcher, E. (1979) *Bottle Collecting* Blandford Press, Poole (5th reprinting)
Litherland, G. (1979) *Bottle Collecting Price Guide* Midlands Antique Bottles Publishing, Burton upon Trent
Martin, L. (1977) *Collectors' Guide to Old Whisky Jugs* L. Martin, London
Masse, H.J.L.J. (1972) *Chats on Old Pewter* Dover Publications
Michaelis, R.F. (1978) *Antique Pewter of the British Isles* Dover Publications Inc.
Morgan, R. (1976) *Sealed Bottles: Their History and Evolution* Midlands Antique Bottles Publishing, Burton upon Trent (2nd edition)
Morgan, R. (1977) *Mainly Codd's Wallop: Story of the Great British Pop Bottle Kollectarama*, Bembridge, I.O.W.
Peal, C.A. (1971) *British Pewter and Britannia Metal* Gifford, London

Tools of the Trade

Craig, W. (1899) *The Cooper Craft*
Crown Cork Company (1966) *Background to the Crown* Crown Cork Company, London
Elkington, G. (1933) *The Coopers' Company and Craft*
Fredericksen, P. (1946) 'Corkscrews that Work' *The Wine Review* Wine Institute of San Francisco
Frith, J.F. (1848) *The Coopers' Company*
Kilby, K. (1971) *The Cooper and His Trade* John Baker, London
Kraus, H. & Babbidge, H.D. (1977) *Symptoms of Withdrawal*
Perry, E. (1980) *Corkscrews and Bottle Openers* Shire Publications, Princes Risborough
Prosser, R.B. (1970) *Birmingham Inventors and Inventions* Country Hist. reprints. S.R. Publishers, Wakefield (Reprint of 1881 edition)

Trade Catalogues

Barthes-Roberts Ltd, Cork Merchants, Brewers' and Bottlers' Sundriesmen, London, 1950
The British Syphon Manufacturing Company Ltd *Standard English Seltzogenes* (*c*.1900) Reprinted by British Syphon Products (Coldflow) Ltd
John Fearn Ltd *Coopers' Tools and Sundries*, Sheffield, *c.* 1960
Gaskell & Chambers Ltd, 1926
T. Heath, Beer Engine Manufacturer, Hotel and Restaurant Bar Fitter, Pewterer and Brass Finisher, London, 1899
W.H. Heath Ltd, Beer Engines and Bar Fitters, London, 1920

Harry Mason Ltd, Birmingham, 1934
Loftus Ltd *Catalogue of Coopers' Tools*, London, *c.*1900

In the Pub

Ayto, E.G. (1979) *Clay Tobacco Pipes* Shire Publications, Princes Risborough
Bryant & May (1961) *Making Matches 1861–1961* Newman Neame Ltd, London
Crowley, T.E. (1975) *Discovering Mechanical Music* Shire Publications, Princes Risborough
Dunhill, A. (1954) *The Gentle Art of Smoking* Alfred Dunhill Ltd, London
Fairhold, F.W. (1876) *Tobacco, its Story and Associations* Chatto & Windus, London
Finn, T. (1960) *Watney Book of Pub Games* Watneys Brewery, London
Finn, T. (1975) *Pub Games of England* Queen Anne Press, London
Gorham, M. & Dunnett (1949) 'Inside the Pub' *Architectural Review* London
Graves, C. (1969) *A Pipe Smoker's Guide* Icon Books Ltd
Griffith, D. (1979) *Decorated Printed Tins* Cassell, London
McCausland, H. (1951) *Snuff and Snuff-Boxes*
Pinto, E.H. (1979) *Treen and Other Wooden Byegones* G. Bell
Player & Sons (1977) *One Hundred Years—the Story of John Player and Sons 1877–1977* John Player Design Studio, Nottingham
Pritchett, R.T. (1890) *Ye Smokiana* Bernard Quartch
Scott, A. & Scott, C. *Tobacco and the Collector*
Steinmetz, A. (1877) *The Smoker's Guide* Hardwich & Bogue, London
Strutt, J. (1801) *Sports and Pastimes of the People of England*
Wilson, J. & Wilson, H. (1968) *The Manufacture of Snuff* Imperial Tobacco Company, London

Miscellaneous Collectables

Bailey, J. (1980) *The Village Blacksmith* Shire Publications, Princes Risborough
Chaney, H.J. (1897) *Our Weights and Measures* Eyre & Spottiswoode
Graham, J.T. (1979) *Weights and Measures* Shire Publications, Princes Risborough
Griffin, A.H. (1950) *The Story of Abbey Horn* Abbey Horn, Kent Works, Kendal
Hart, E. (1979) *The Heavy Horse* Shire Publications, Princes Risborough
Keegan, T. (1973) *The Heavy Horse: Its Harness and Harness Decoration* Pelham Books, London

Keegan, T. (1978) *Harness Decorations* Keegan, The Oxleys, Claws Top, Nr Kidderminster

Keegan, T. (1981) *Take a Seat—The Cast Iron Seats of Great Britain* Keegan, The Oxleys, Claws Top, Nr Kidderminster

Larwood, J. & Hotten, J.C. (1866) *The History of Signboards from the Earliest Times to the Present Day* Hotten, London

Neumann, J. (1858) *Beschreibung der Bekanntesten Kupfermunzen* [Description of the most well-known copper coins] Volumes 1 to 6 (Reprinted 1966)

Quinion, M. (1982) *Cidermaking* Shire Publications, Princes Risborough

Thompson, J. (1977–79) *Horse Drawn Farm Implements: Volume 1 Ploughs; Volume 2 Preparing the Soil; Volume 3 Sowing and Haymaking; Volume 4 Harvesting* John Thompson, Fleet

Thompson, J. (1977) *Horse-Drawn Heavy Goods Vehicles* John Thompson, Fleet

Thompson, J. (1977) *Horse-Drawn Trade Vehicles* John Thompson, Fleet

Todd, N.B. (1979) *British and Irish Tokens 1830–1920* (2nd edition)

Tylden, G. (1971) *Discovering Harness and Saddlery* Shire Publications, Princes Risborough

Vince, J. (1968) *Discovering Horse Brasses* Shire Publications, Princes Risborough

Vince, J. (1982) *Old Farm Tools* Shire Publications, Princes Risborough

Vipan, J.A.M. (1908) *Coins, Medals & Local Tradesmen's Tokens . . . in the Peterborough Museum* Lincolnshire Museums

Some Notable Pubs and Museums

A.B.C. Travel (1982) *Museums and Galleries in Great Britain and Ireland* A.B.C., Dunstable

Burke, J. (1981) *The English Inn* Batsford, London

Davis, B. (1981) *The Traditional English Pub* Architectural Press, London

Matz, B. (1921) *Inns & Taverns of 'Pickwick'* Cecil Palmer, London

Matz, B. (1922) *Dickensian Inns & Taverns* Cecil Palmer, London

National Trust (1980) *Country House Treasures* Weidenfeld and Nicolson, London

Protz, R., ed. (1980) *Campaign For Real Ale. Good Beer Guide* CAMRA/Arrow Books Ltd, London

Spiller, B. (1976) *Victorian Public Houses* David & Charles, Newton Abbot (New edition)

Tester & Henabary (1979) *English Pubs Through American Eyes* HAT Enterprise, Cookstown, New Jersey, USA/The Red Lion, Steeple Aston, Oxfordshire

Trade Catalogues

See under Tools of the Trade

Periodicals

The Breweriana Collector Journal of the National Association of Breweriana Advertising

Exchange and Mart Link House, Poole, Dorset. Weekly

Finders Keepers Monthly. From Kollectarama, 6 High Street, Bembridge, I.O.W.

The Heavy Horse Quarterly from Woodside House, Pembory, Kent

The Huntsman Quarterly from Joshua Tetley & Son Ltd, Leeds

Top Hat Bi-annual journal of the Burtonwood Brewery Co. Ltd, Warrington, Cheshire

W. & D.B. News Quarterly from Wolverhampton & Dudley Breweries Ltd, Wolverhampton, Staffordshire

What's Brewing Monthly journal of the Campaign for Real Ale

Index